Howards' Way

Howards' Way

GERARD GLAISTER and RAY EVANS

BBC BOOKS

This book could not have been written without the generous help of the cast and production team of *Howards' Way*.

Thanks, too, to Tony Castro, the real-life designer of Barracuda and Spring; and to Chris Collman, of Quay Marine, Hamble.

Picture credits

Cover picture of a Spring © Patrick Roach. All other colour pictures are © BBC Enterprises except; a Barracuda moored and in action before transatlantic yacht race, Abby being made-up & pictures of Leo & Emma on location which are all © Kos Photos; a Barracuda under full sail © Sadler Yachts Ltd; a Spring under full sail © Patrick Roach; Avril & Charles admiring Anna Lee's designs © Jim Hatchard and Tom signing autographs © Bella Magazine (photo by Kos).

All black and white pictures are © BBC Enterprises except; pages 3 & 119 (left) Kos Photos; 12 (left), 75, 126 & 145 Gerard Glaister; 63 (below), 112 & 140 Jim Hatchard; 61 & 114 Bryan Drew Ltd; 71 Brunskill Management; 77 Susan Angel Associates; 81 Artefact Associates; 91 Kate Feast Management; 92 Neil Wigley; 98 MLR; 104 Larry Dalzell Associates Ltd; 107 Green & Underwood Ltd; 110 April Young Ltd; 117 Crouch Associates; 119 (right) Bella Magazine (photo by Kos); 125 Gerry Walden Studios and 159 Photochrome Audio Visual.

Published by BBC Books, a division of BBC Enterprises Limited, Woodlands, 80 Wood Lane, London W12 0TT

First published 1988   © Gerard Glaister and Ray Evans 1988   Preface © Gerard Glaister 1988

ISBN 0 563 20712 4

Set in 12/15pt Optima and printed and bound in Great Britain by Butler and Tanner Ltd, Frome
Colour separations by Technik, Berkhamsted
Colour printing by Chorley and Pickersgill Ltd, Leeds
Jacket printed by Fletchers Ltd, Northampton

CONTENTS

CAST LIST

SERIES 1 (1985)   SERIES 2 (1986)   SERIES 3 (1987)   SERIES 4 (1988)

Character	Actor	Series no
Tom Howard	Maurice Colbourne	all
Jan Howard	Jan Harvey	all
Leo Howard	Edward Highmore	all
Lynne Howard	Tracey Childs	1,2
Kate Harvey	Dulcie Gray	all
Jack Rolfe	Glyn Owen	all
Avril Rolfe	Susan Gilmore	all
Ken Masters	Stephen Yardley	all
Charles Frere	Tony Anholt	all
Sir Edward Frere	Nigel Davenport	3 on
Gerald Urquhart	Ivor Danvers	all
Polly Urquhart	Patricia Shakesby	all
Abby Urquhart	Cindy Shelley	all
Claude Dupont	Malcolm Jamieson	1,2
Dawn	Sally Farmiloe	1,2
Sarah Foster	Sarah-Jane Varley	2 on
Mark Foster	Graham Poutney	2,3
Richard Shellet	Oscar Quitak	1,2
Emma Newsome	Sian Webber	3 on
Davy	Kulvinder Ghir	1,2
Bill Sayers	Robert Vahey	all
Orrin Hudson	Ryan Michael	2
Sir John Stevens	Willoughby Grey	all
Curtis Jaeger	Dean Harris	2
David Lloyd	Bruce Bould	all
Amanda Parker	Francesca Gonshaw	3
Anna Lee	Sarah Lam	3
Richard Spencer	John Moulder-Brown	3
Michael Hanley	Michael Loney	3 on

PREFACE

To make a television programme requires a team of people, working closely together, believing in what they are trying to create. I was fortunate to have a magnificent team. My artists have worked together wonderfully well as a unit for four years. They support each other at all times. The creative work of the writers has contributed considerably to the success of the programme. I could not have asked for better camera crews, both film and video. The designers have been dedicated to the programme and contributed immensely to its glossy look. My directors have conformed to the style and created more than I could have hoped for at the outset. All the back-up personnel on the unit have worked unselfishly to produce the kind of programme I asked for. The costume designers and the make-up artists have given me wonderful support. Altogether I have been a lucky man to have had such a fine unit to work with.

I must add that my secretary, Yvonne Alfert, worked all hours, looking after fan mail for the cast, arranging photographs for the many people who wrote in, coping with the press enquiries. The perfect Girl Friday.

Altogether, the programme has occupied my life for the past six years. They have been most enjoyable years.

Gerard Glaister

CHAPTER ONE

Laying the Keel

~~~

'It isn't going to work, is it?'

Gerard Glaister and his agent, Robin Lowe, leant despondently on a rail and looked across the ranks of yachts at the Boat Show. All of them had fibre-glass hulls; and where they could see the honey glow of wood, it was only from cabin doors and interiors. There wasn't a wooden boat to be seen, and that was the problem.

The idea for a series about boatbuilders had stemmed from a lunch Gerry had had with Jonathan Powell, the brilliant young producer of the TV adaptations of John le Carré's novels, who had recently been appointed the BBC's Head of Series and Serials and is now Controller of BBC 1. At the time, Powell was looking for a new serial along the lines of *The Brothers*, which Gerry had produced. Something to go into the autumn drama list for Sunday evenings, which would attract an audience of eleven million people. A tall order, but Powell had come to the right man. Gerry had a string of BBC credits which read like a roll of honour: his most recent productions included *Colditz*, *Secret Army*, *Kessler* and *Cold Warrior*.

Two things were needed to give a new drama serial fresh angles and originality. The first was to interweave the work background more than it had been in other serials, apart from those set in workplaces which directly reflected the drama, such as hospitals and police stations. In *The Brothers*, the road-haulage business was merely a background, just as the oil business is in *Dallas*; but boatbuilding was much more visually attractive and interesting than lorries or oil. Plenty of people would relate to it, because nearly everybody likes boats, and thousands own them – from simple dinghies to luxury cruisers – and boat ownership is on the increase. As the idea for the serial took root, a mix was agreed of one-third boats, one-third business, and one-third personal relationships.

The second element was to replace the familiar locations of kitchen, back garden, corner-shop and public bar. The world of boats would get the actors and the action out of doors, and into a world no less real than that of the terraced provincial street or Cockney pub, but which hadn't been seen so much: the world of the wealthy, who live well, who are successful and who can afford a more glamorous life than most of us. Without failure and the danger of failure there is no drama; but adversity doesn't always mean a shortage of money.

There is much more reality in the whole serial than is often supposed. The characters reflect real types in their material and social standing, and the sort of world in which they move. Some time ago a television team did a survey in the Southampton area to find out people's reactions to *Howards' Way*. Hoping for some adverse reaction they approached a man in a blue blazer who looked as though he might be a member of the local sailing establishment. Much to their disappointment, they got this reply: 'Well, they build the boats a bit quicker than it'd take in real life, but on the whole you could say that *Howards' Way* is our way.'

Yachts and boatbuilding were first suggested by Gerry as a backdrop for a drama serial when he was discussing the format of *The Brothers* with N. J. Crisp sixteen years earlier. It wasn't used then, but the idea stayed at the back of his mind, partly because yachts are so beautiful. After the lunch with Jonathan Powell, he saw how boatbuilding and the two new elements could be made to fit together. The setting and the locations would have to be dead right. A small boatyard was needed, where wooden boats were still made and where a relatively small cast of characters could be introduced. The problem with glass-fibre boats was that they were produced in factories and their hulls were pressed from a mould. In *Howards' Way*, Relton Marine produces hulls like this, and has another factory up the road where bathtubs are produced by a similar process. So for all their advantages – cheaper to make and buy, easier to maintain, lighter in weight – and for all that craftsmen do fit them out in wood, glass-fibre boats don't have the interest of wooden ones in the building process. Gerry wanted to film men laying a keel, but despite the boom in the yachting industry, it is the production-line boats that are on the increase. Even the most traditional boatbuilder must move with the times or go out of business. Which is why Gerry was depressed when he visited the Boat Show.

There was another difficulty. Even if he found a traditional builder, the boatyard couldn't be just anywhere. For practical reasons, it had to be within easy reach of London, and have good hotel accommodation for the cast and crew. It would have to be accessible from Birmingham, too, where the studio sequences would be shot and where many of the production team were based.

The south coast seemed the best bet, and somewhere on the Solent best of all. The problem was where? The location was so important that if he couldn't find the right one, he might as well forget the whole thing. Gerry knew what he wanted, but had no experience of sailing, and no contacts in the field. Then his wife Joan remembered that a friend who'd worked with her at the BBC had married a colleague who had these contacts. Bob Fisher was now a freelance yachting correspondent and professional sailor, based in Lymington.

Soon afterwards Gerry was outlining his plans and his needs to Bob at the Royal Ocean Racing Club in London; a couple of weeks later Bob rang to suggest that they meet in Southampton: 'I've got some locations to show you but there's something else I want you to see first.'

Gerry drove down and agreed to follow Bob. 'Following Bob is like tailing a Grand Prix driver. Fortunately it was a Sunday morning and the roads were quite clear. Bob is an energetic and impatient man who likes to get on with things quickly; it was obvious that to him time spent driving was time wasted. Finally we reached the village of Bursledon, drove on to the wide bridge across the Hamble and stopped. We got out and he pointed downstream towards the sea. I knew it was the right place from

Below Producer
Gerard Glaister

the word go. It was magnificent – hundreds and hundreds of yachts, a forest of masts; and the clatter of the stays in the wind.'

Bob pointed out a boatyard about two hundred metres downstream on the right bank. It was a small place, a bit ramshackle, but cluttered with boats. 'It's called the Elephant Yard. Family run. People called Richardson.'

Gerry knew he'd found what he was after; and a closer look wasn't disappointing. 'We turned off the main road and drove down a winding lane for half a mile or so, and came to a halt by a low brick wall. From there we walked down a steep slope to the boatyard. From what I could see, it looked as if repairs and refurbishment were the bread-and-butter work; but when we got to the workshop I knew this was the central location I wanted. They were building a wooden boat.' The Mermaid Yard was born.

Left 'A forest of masts'
Below On the Hamble

Howards' Way was developed not from the characters, but from the location. All Gerry originally had in mind was a family and boatbuilding, so things proceeded the other way round from the usual course, which begins with the characters. In a sense, though, the locations were characters too. 'I was lucky to have found in Bob Fisher the person who knew every boatyard on the south coast,' says Gerry. 'And by luck the area we use, around the mouth of the Hamble, turned out to have nearly every location we needed, all close to one another.

This is of practical importance because although filming is on 16mm, not 35mm, it is still a very expensive business. An average filming day on *Howards' Way* costs £5000, and travelling between locations wastes time. However, the fictional town of Tarrant has boundaries which are deliberately blurred, and the places which make it up are not all in Bursledon and Lymington, the towns either side of Southampton which are the principal filming areas.

Once the locations were identified, even though no formal arrangements were made at that stage with their owners, Gerry felt he could go ahead and develop the format. He teamed up with the writer Allan Prior but the process was slow. They finally produced a 'selling document' to show Jonathan Powell, who was convinced that the project should go ahead. Prior produced a pilot script, which again was okayed by Powell. The serial was to be called *The Boatbuilders*. Gerry was now able to get his team together.

One principle Gerry firmly believes in is that of the producer as benevolent dictator. He is not dictatorial in any obvious sense, but he feels that only one person can make the final decisions if the 'house style' of a programme is to be consistent. In what was by now *Howards' Way*, since the name of the principal family had been decided, a definite unity of style is easy to see – but it goes further than dovetailing characters with the clothes they wear, the cars they drive, the places they live, and the music which supports them. The style extends to the way the programme is shot. There are no long panning shots, and no pandering to scenic backgrounds – when they are there they are integrated. Shots are kept tight, angles interesting. The action moves forward all the time, and the charac-

ters are never static (as they are in *Dallas*, for example, where experience never changes them) but develop, whatever the consequences; which means that, unlike many open-ended sagas, they do not fall into the trap of endless repetition.

Music is specially composed for each episode. Several characters – Abby, and Sir Edward, for example – have their own themes. The opening and closing music has been changed for each of the first three series. In series two, the original theme was rearranged as a wistful ballad, sung by Marti Webb, to reflect the romance and sadness of the main stories. In series three, the brisker tempo of the Barracuda theme reflected the harder world of business as Jan Howard and Ken Masters work their way up the ladder, and as Charles Frere locks horns with his father.

Marti Webb's record of the theme song for series 2

ALWAYS THERE
plus HOWARDS' WAY original theme

MARTI WEBB
with
THE SIMON MAY ORCHESTRA

Design is vital in a drama whose characters are conscious of taste. A team was needed who would enjoy what they were doing and go for the glossy image of the new affluence and its visual and entertainment values. One consideration in casting the actors and actresses was not only that they should look their parts but that they should be able to wear clothes well – especially the women. As generous a slice as possible of the budget of £3 million per series goes to design. The costume designers are able to buy top-of-the-range clothes; and, for the designer dresses that Polly, Jan and Avril wear from the 'collections' of Claude Dupont and Anna Lee, Yuki, Alistair Blair, Bruce Oldfield and Jeff Banks, among others, have been delighted to lend models.

Along with the glamour has come a good deal of interest from the tabloids and buckets of mud have been slung, mainly inaccurately, by *The Sun* and *The News of the World*. It's true that off-screen two marriages came to an end, and during the last series an actress had an affair with a director (no longer working on the show) who subsequently went back to his wife. But that's about all, although there is a local joke: 'Are you married or do you live in Tarrant?'

Gerry is philosophical: 'For some reason, *Howards' Way* has been more plagued by the popular press than any other serial I've worked on. On the other hand nobody split up to live with someone else on any of the other serials. When the press ask me about my actors, I say, "As long as they turn up on time, know their lines, and don't trip over the furniture, their private lives are their own affair." ' Being in the public eye and in a serial where there has been some partner-swapping, the cast are bound to have their private lives exposed to public scrutiny more than the average man or woman; but they aren't necessarily any more venal. The two long marriages that ended would have ended anyway, and it's not the people who appear on television who are hurt by the publicity – as Stephen Yardley, who was on the receiving end of some of it, pointed out. It's their relatives and their children who have to put up with the looks and the questions, whether it's at school or the local shop. Stephen was relatively

Stephen Yardley on location

lucky – his wife refused to talk to the press. All the main actors and actresses now have steady relationships (touch wood). As for the past, it is sad but not unusual for people to split up!

No one, in terms of letters from 'Disgusted, Tunbridge Wells', has batted an eyelid about any of the on-screen stories which might have seemed to sail close to the wind: Richard Shellet's incestuous love for his sister, Jack Rolfe's late wife; Charles Frere's cynical seduction of Lynne, a girl young enough to be his daughter; Mark Foster's suicide when he discovers his wife's infidelity (and more, the speed with which she recovers from it); and the revelation that Gerald Urquhart is gay (which came as quite a shock to the actor). The only scene which stirred strong emotions and jammed the switchboards showed a group of men preparing two terriers for a dogfight. 'How dare you show two innocent animals tearing each other apart' was the line, but nothing of the sort was shown. Before it could start, the fight was broken up by Curtis Jaeger, an animal activist with whom the confused Abby had a brief affair. The setting-up of the scene was authentically researched through the RSPCA, and an RSPCA inspector was present throughout its filming.

There have been other upsets. Claude Dupont's death in a water-skiing accident – he was in the water and was hit by a speedboat towing another skier – was objected to by various water-skiing organisations. They said it was inaccurate to show a towing-boat with only a driver aboard, and no observer to look out in the direction the boat was going. There is no law, however, to enforce such practice, and in 1986 a swimmer was killed in similar circumstances to those in which Claude 'died'.

Then there was the trouble over the *Lynette*, the story of the catamaran disaster which was to plunge Tom Howard into almost certain ruin. David Alan-Williams and Ian King, the designer and builder of *Alien*, the catamaran which had actually been used for the story, not surprisingly became very worried that their reputation and that of their boat would suffer if the fictional catamaran broke up as the result of a design fault. Jim Hatchard, designer on *Howards' Way* for the past three years, was directly involved. He'd been given a sheaf of scripts which called for a wonderful, offbeat, futuristic catamaran, and found *Alien*. Her makers were happy to lend her, as at that time there was no clue as to how the story would develop. But even when it was clear that in the story the design of the boat might be called into question, they allowed Jim to paint a fake stress fracture on her hull. Later, when things were at their grimmest, they lent him the drawings for *Alien* so that he could design the section of broken hull used after the fictional accident. Most of the misunderstanding stemmed from uncertainty about how the story would resolve itself, of course; and once the *Lynette* was exonerated (it was fellow boat designer Tony Castro who suggested that she broke up after hitting an underwater object), the fuss died down. Not that there weren't unpleasant moments for Jim. 'I went into one of the local pubs down there at the time and an associate of Ian's actually walked out.' Jim has remained good friends with Alan and Ian, and has sailed on *Alien* with them since. She is a beautiful boat, and she is still sailing perfectly safely. As for Jim, his association with *Howards' Way* has turned him into a keen sailor: 'I'm a future yachtie, no doubt of that.'

The Jolly Sailor with the *Lynette* in the foreground

The same is not true of the serial's producer. His lifetime hobby is fly-fishing, and he has not been converted despite the vast amount of sailing knowledge he's acquired. He has landed salmon up to 25lbs from a bank of the Dee, where he tries to get away from the non-stop demands of *Howards' Way*. A dozen rods hang in his study, and he has tied every one of his collection of flies himself. Although Scottish by ancestry, Gerry Glaister was born in Hong Kong, 'though I left when I was six months old'. There is something of a Far East connection in the programme: Dulcie Gray was born in Kuala Lumpur; Tony Anholt in Singapore; and Patricia Shakesby's sister is married to the Director of Museums for Malaysia.

The 1988 series features the annual international power boat race at Guernsey, in which Leo takes part as a driver. When Gerry was over in St Peter Port to discuss the filming, a local journalist asked him if he had ever been there before. 'Yes, when I bombed it!' he replied. He was in the RAF during the war and flew Blenheim bombers over Europe. He made forty-five sorties at a time when the average 'life expectancy' was six. Later, he flew Spitfires out of Egypt on reconnaissance over the Mediterranean. He earned a DFC. He comes from a medical family. His uncle was professor of forensic medicine at Glasgow University, succeeding his grandfather, who held the same chair. They kept the professorship in the family for sixty-six years. Gerry's uncle also practised as a lawyer, and Erle Stanley Gardner, creator of Perry Mason, used to send him a case of whisky every year for indirectly providing him with many good plots. Gerry also developed the first of the series and serials he was to devise and produce from conversations with his uncle. It was called *The Expert*, the first colour series done by the BBC, and was, not surprisingly, about a forensic scientist.

Every new project presents a new set of problems, but *Howards' Way* is particularly complex. The many technical difficulties and intricacies of scheduling any television drama are compounded by the tides, the availability of boats, teaching actors to sail and so on. With the short and unreliable English summer, the weather can be a continual headache, though the camera makes things look brighter than they are. Sarah-Jane

Varley remembers a scene where she lounges in the open cockpit of a cruiser, dressed in a bikini and sipping champagne in the sun. In fact there was a steady drizzle and she was blue with cold.

Plenty of people shook their heads at the difficulty of getting the show on at all, but Gerry thinks that the only way is to get on and do the thing as best you can. That way many of the apparent problems disappear. He recalls the difficulties of making *Colditz* – the castle is now in East Germany. He negotiated two days' filming with the authorities there, and went and took a number of establishing shots himself. They built the first two floors of the castle as a set in the big studios at Ealing, and whenever an actor walked across it and had to look up they cut to the film Gerry had taken of the upper half of Colditz. 'Never say, this is too difficult, we can't do it; say instead, this is very difficult, how can we do it? And then just get on with it, and keep your cool.'

CHAPTER TWO

Raising the Mast

~~~~

The story of *Howards' Way* started with the Howard family. Tom, Jan, and their children Lynne and Leo, live in the affluent community of Tarrant, on the banks of the River Hamble, in Hampshire. The river is dominated by boats – yachts and pleasure cruisers – and most of the locals are more or less connected with them for their livelihood.

The same can be said for many of those who live in the real towns of Bursledon and Lymington, where a view across the marina shows no sign of an economic recession. You can hardly see the water for sailing boats, motor cruisers and dinghies. There is no doubt that this is one of the most prosperous corners of Britain, and that as long as the prosperity continues the pleasure-boat industry will maintain its present renaissance. *Howards' Way* mirrors what already exists, and has also indirectly encouraged its expansion; and although the characters of the serial are fictitious, they are not at all far from people you could meet in the Southampton area, or in the pubs and yacht clubs of Lymington and Bursledon.

Tom has worked all his life for Southern Aviation and has reached the position of senior designer when the company merges with another and he is made redundant. A keen sailor, who has designed his own boat and seen it built, Tom breaks the bad news to his family during a celebration dinner to mark his victory in a yacht race. Although both his children are keen sailors, especially Lynne, his wife Jan has no interest in yachting. She is appalled at his decision to use his generous redundancy money to go into the boat business for himself, and is even more distressed that at no

Far left The Howard family. *Left* On board the *Flying Fish*. *Below left* Chez Howard

point does he consult her or bring her into his decision-making. She has always been the wife and mother; he has always been the breadwinner. That was Tom's attitude, and Jan accepted it – but Tom's redundancy is destined to change those roles and their view of life.

Despite being warned against it, Tom buys into the Mermaid Boatyard, which is run by a brilliant boatbuilder, Jack Rolfe. Though he knows about boats Jack is no businessman, refuses to move with the times, and is well on the way to becoming an alcoholic. Tom's stubbornness causes the cracks already present in his marriage to widen, and he and Jan part. She goes to work part-time for a local entrepreneur, Ken Masters, who has a yacht chandlery. Ken, a cockney with an instinct for business, is climbing the ladder of success fast, and his fascination for Jan is largely due to the fact that she is 'classy'. Jan is vaguely aware that he is attracted to her personally, but for the moment is pleased to find that she enjoys and adapts well to the world of business, which up until now she has had little or no experience of.

Jack Rolfe tucks into a pint at The Jolly Sailor

Ken and Jan in the chandlery

As for the children, Leo abandons plans to go to university – he'd never wanted to go anyway – and to Jan's annoyance he gets a lowly job as a pump attendant at one of Ken Masters' chain of garages. However, the association with Masters will stand him in good stead, and his career will remain closely and successfully linked to that of the man who becomes his mother's lover for a time, and who seems determined to marry her if she will ever have him. Leo, who is disinclined to become one of Tarrant's 'bright young things', finds a friend in the desperately unhappy misfit, Abby Urquhart. Abby is a poor little rich girl – unable to love or understand her brittle, facile mother or make contact with her remote, preoccupied father. She has just come home from finishing school in Switzerland distinctly unpolished, acutely depressed and pregnant.

A penny for your thoughts, Abby . . .

Below Tom and Avril discuss a problem in the Mermaid office. *Right* Lynne

Tom has to sell his boat, the *Flying Fish*, to raise the money to buy into the boatyard, and this upsets Lynne. She takes a job as a barmaid at the local yacht club – to Tom's disgust – but her motives are simply to sniff out any possibilities of crewing for other yacht owners. She ends up crewing on an all-female entry in the Fastnet race, in which she acquits herself with honour. She goes on with her sailing career, first by vindicating her father's design of the *Barracuda of Tarrant* by sailing it single-handed across the Atlantic, and then by joining Jo Penhaligon, the skipper of the Fastnet boat, to run a sailing school in Italy. She still keeps in touch with her family and friends in Tarrant.

Meanwhile, at the boatyard Tom strikes up a friendship with Jack's daughter Avril, a woman with good business sense herself, who sees what

a boon Tom will be to the Mermaid. She sides with him against her father on the question of introducing new designs, materials and techniques. Avril is back in Tarrant from London after a bust-up with a long-term lover (Charles Frere) and, in view of their emotional states, the alliance between Tom and Avril quickly escalates into something much closer. Unfortunately Leo has also had quite a crush on Avril, so when he discovers what's actually going on, he is shattered – but he grows through the experience and, if anything, it subsequently brings him closer to his father.

While the members of the Howard family find their feet in their new roles, each in turn finds some sort of support in Jan's mother. An ideal universal mum – kindly, experienced, practical, but not intrusive – Kate Harvey hides her own grief at the break-up of her daughter's marriage, supports her adored ex-son-in-law, and even finds time to help Jack Rolfe on the first few steps of his battle with the bottle, after finding him tottering along the road drunk one evening.

RAISING THE MAST | 29

Mother and daughter. Jan confides her problems in Kate

The Frere family is small – the widowed multi-millionaire, Sir Edward, and his son, Charles, scarcely less rich – and they are at loggerheads. Sir Edward wants Charles to work for him; Charles does not want to be part of his father's empire or in his father's power in any way. Indeed, his ambition, if anything, is to break him. Despite their disunited front the two men have a profound effect on Tarrant and the other main characters of *Howards' Way*. When Charles moves into the area, Avril is unable to resist him, and leaves Tom to return to him. Sir Edward woos Jan – unsuccessfully in the end, but seriously enough to shake her; and it is through his good offices that she has acquired enough capital to expand the brilliantly successful fashion house which she started from modest beginnings with Ken Masters' help.

Tom has a rockier ride up the ladder of success. Constantly hamstrung by Jack Rolfe's conservatism, and initially dogged by ill-luck in his boat designs, he is now beginning to see the light of day. After the disastrous accident involving his new catamaran, the *Lynette*, the boat and its design have been fully vindicated by the enquiry, and have brought Tom a new lover in the form of the gorgeous marine scientist, Emma Newsome (played by Sian Webber). However, Charles Frere had bought out the company due to develop Tom's other design, the Ultra-Light Displacement Boat (ULDB), *Barracuda*, and was unwilling to go into production even after the *Lynette*'s name was cleared. Only Avril, who Charles had by now made managing director of the company involved, Relton Marine, was able to save the day. With her help, and Lynne's courageous transatlantic voyage, Tom was able to get out of the doldrums into which he had veered. Now, even Jack is coming round to the new methods. With two new boats to follow *Barracuda*, the wind looks set fair for the Mermaid to survive financially and fight off the depredations of Charles Frere.

The other family involved in Charles Frere's sphere of influence are the Urquharts, whose unhappy daughter Abby, transformed by motherhood and an ill-advised marriage in the States to the American father of her son William, will almost certainly end up with Leo, her supporter and loyal friend since early in the first series. Gerald Urquhart is a lawyer and accountant whose chief client is Charles Frere. Indeed, we might assume

Gerald listens as
Charles outlines
strategy

Polly

Opposite page
The family that never
was – Orrin, Abby and
baby Michael

that he is wholly retained by Frere, who sometimes treats him very badly indeed; but also with the kindness and great friendship that he feels for him deep down.

The men were at Cambridge together, and it was there that Charles slept with Polly, another undergraduate, and made her pregnant – with Abby. Gerald, a homosexual, stepped into the breach to save Polly's reputation and cover his own – he was going into the City at a time when he would not have prospered had his homosexuality been discovered; at the time did not know who Abby's father was. He and Polly have muddled through twenty years of marriage, sexually frustrating on both sides, and they have achieved a basic friendship and mutual regard which has seen them through some very rough water recently and on to a new understanding. This is particularly poignant as they do not 'need' each other practically any more, with Abby grown up, the divorce-rate so high as barely to merit a second glance socially, and Gerald established enough to withstand any smear – itself unlikely in a more relaxed society than the one he grew up in. What the future holds for them we do not know.

But perhaps it was Lynne Howard who was most personally affected by Charles's arrival in Tarrant. She fell for him, and one night he seduced her on his motor cruiser. The affair continued and grew, and Lynne began to think that despite his being an urbane cosmopolitan twice her age, it might be serious. When Charles cooled, Lynne unwisely chased him, and one night she went to his boat unannounced, to surprise him in bed with another woman.

Two affairs in real life between *Howards' Way* actors have attracted the attention of the press, both mirroring affairs in the series, and both, unlike those in the series, ending happily for those concerned. One is between Jan Harvey and Stephen Yardley (Jan Howard and Ken Masters);

Together? Ken and Jan

the other between Tony Anholt and Tracey Childs (Charles and Lynne). In the series, Lynne recovers from the trauma of Charles's betrayal to fall for Claude Dupont, the handsome French designer who works for her mother. They marry, but only a short time after he is tragically killed in a water-skiing accident. It was then that Lynne took herself off to Italy, to get away from the scene of so much unhappiness and try to start a new life centred on her first real love – sailing. In fact, Tracey Childs wanted to leave the series because there was a strong chance that she would be getting an important film role. In the way of these things, it didn't materialise after all, but she has appeared recently in the daytime soap opera *Gems*. Whether Lynne will ever return to Tarrant remains an open question.

Ken Masters, like Jan Howard, goes from strength to strength, successful in everything he does except in his pursuit of her. But in going public he is entering the most ambitious and dangerous phase of his career so far. He has stretched himself to the limit, and he has done so on the very dubious advice of a consultant already suborned by Sir Edward Frere, who wishes to break him. Meanwhile, although he is the driving force behind his company, Leisurecruise, he is not the majority shareholder. She is the stunningly beautiful Sarah Foster, played by Sarah-Jane Varley, whose affair with him led to her husband's suicide, and who is, to say the least, a very uneasy ally. At the moment though, Ken basks. He is a paper millionaire, and he is at the wheel of his very own Rolls-Royce. In his own mind, he has arrived – but has he? Series four will see reversals of fortune for many – for good and for bad.

All the principal characters and their occupations were thought out in advance by Gerry and his original script editor, veteran film and television writer John Brason. These character studies go right back to the 'lives' they had before the series began. Thus we know that Jack Rolfe is the son of a small farmer, and that Charles, Gerald and Polly were all up at Cambridge together. It's important for a scriptwriter to have some foundation on which to build and, as in real life, the characters must occasionally refer to their pasts.

They are designed as carefully as everything else to fit in with the unity that distinguishes *Howards' Way*. For example, Gerry thought it very important to introduce contemporary women who could hold their own and run their own businesses – hence the characters of Jan and Avril. '*Howards' Way* is entertainment,' he says; 'and made as entertainment – the equivalent, if you like, of the good light novel people would read for relaxation before the advent of television; but that doesn't mean we can't imply real points about the society we live in.'

Jan runs her fashion house, and Avril runs Relton's. In real life, two very successful recent business ventures – Pineapple and The Body Shop – have been headed by women. In the future, we may see Jan diversifying as her business grows, in the same way as did Mary Quant and Laura Ashley, but an important thing about Jan is that her business acumen has become apparent to her only in early middle age. Her first job was as a secretary at Southern Aviation, where she met Tom. There followed twenty years as a wife and mother.

The link between Tom Howard taking up yacht design and his aircraft design training and background is also based on real experience. Many of Gerry's old RAF friends and colleagues were also keen yachtsmen. Flying and sailing have more in common than flying and driving, scientifically as well as emotionally. The Elephant Yard's most recent purchaser, the present owner's father, took it over after being made redundant from the aircraft industry in the early fifties. The transition from aircraft design to boat design, too, is not hard to make, because the aerodynamic problems and considerations are the same. It was logical to prepare the ground for Tom's change of career, once the overall storyline for series one had been agreed, by making him a keen sailor already and the designer of his own boat, *Flying Fish*. In reality the yacht is a Laser 28, a Canadian design sold here by Performance Sailcraft Europe Ltd. It is now rarely used in the series but has always featured in the opening credits.

Tom's character is also based on authentic precedents. It's feasible for a man of his background to invest his golden handshake in a business of his own. In the eighties disillusionment with working for people, and the relative insecurity of being an employee have become hard realities.

With the Mermaid Yard as the centre of interest, dramatic conflict there had to be worked out carefully and to evolve naturally, as it does if it is any good at all, out of the characters. Tom has business sense, which Jack fundamentally does not. Jack is a romantic and a perfectionist, who will always want to build wooden boats and build them as works of art, without regard for deadlines and cash-flow. Tom wants the help of modern technology and to make money and prestige out of what he does. Sometimes he overreaches himself, but without him Jack would have gone under long ago. Of course there is some licence here, since the traditional boatbuilder today not only tolerates high-tech but welcomes its advantages. He'd have a hard struggle to compete if he didn't. Jack is slowly coming round, but he's not won over yet.

The boatbuilders

The Howards and the Rolfes were the first characters to be invented; others went through radical changes before they reached the screen. Kate Harvey, Jan's mother, was originally conceived as a grand*father*. They made the sex change because they wanted to use the character as a sounding-board for the teenage Howard children, Leo and Lynne. A bonus was the relationship they later developed between Kate and Jack. Charles Frere was brought in as a villain, but his lines were quickly softened as there was no desire to introduce a character as two-dimensional as J.R. Charles's character reflects the serious big business interest there is on the south coast, where a surprising amount of money is in circulation and where such ventures as business parks are under development. His motivation for coming back to the area is threefold: he was born there, so his roots are

Charles Frere – driving force or driven man?

there, and his father has a large house in the neighbourhood; he also wants to see what business opportunities there are, since he is a natural entrepreneur. Lastly, he cannot shake off his feelings for Avril Rolfe, who has moved back there after he ditched her in London. Recently, we've got to know more of the real man behind the ruthless exterior.

As we have seen, the characters stemmed from the locations. Relatively late arrivals were Kate and Abby, who was introduced as Polly's daughter at the suggestion of John Brason. John also invented Jack Rolfe's manic brother-in-law, Richard Shellet, a Gothic character who worked extremely well, and through whom we were able to see Jack beyond the bluster. As we have also said, they and their relationships develop as they would in real life, wherever that may lead (one of the usual dreads of an open-ended serial producer is a story which must end in a principal actor leaving). In this, *Howards' Way* has an advantage over soap operas, which have to carry on at least twice-weekly throughout the year, but it is still rare to see such development in other serials of the same type.

The characters are all highly motivated in what they do – for example, Charles Frere is keen to outdo his father because he grew up in his shadow; and Ken desperately wants to be part of the establishment. However, characters still serve the plot. 'The reason that I killed off Claude was that I could see no further use for him,' Gerry says. 'He'd had his big romance, he'd married, and there was really nowhere else for him to go. We already knew that Tracey Childs was leaving the series in the hope of a film part, you see; so we made a dramatic point of Claude's death.' Similarly, Amanda Parker served her purpose in being part of the process of Leo's growing up. There was no way he was going to remain tied to her, especially as we probably all know whom he's destined to end up with! Even if the character of Amanda hadn't been unpopular with the viewers, which she was, she would not have returned.

We have seen how the settings shaped the characters and how they were developed, but before finding out how they were cast, let us look at the life-stories of some of the inhabitants of Tarrant.

TOM HOWARD

Tom was born in 1941, and until recently he worked as a design engineer with Southern Aviation. His father, Frank, lived in Warwickshire, and started working life as a jobbing carpenter. Later on, he managed to set up in business for himself making furniture. The business prospered until the interruption of the Second World War which soon brought things to a standstill.

Tom's mother Jenny was, at thirty-six, already in early middle age when she gave birth to him. After the war, when Tom was four, Frank started the business up once again, but the persistent shortage of materials, and the arrival of cheap ready-made furniture, made it impossible to carry on. He was forced to close down the business and return to being a carpenter. However, Tom was brought up in a family which, though never rich, never lacked the essentials either. He turned out to be an eager and intelligent pupil at primary school and passed his eleven-plus. From grammar school he went on to a redbrick university and took a B.Sc. in Aeronautics. He joined Southern Aviation in 1964 and went straight into the design department. There he remained, making steady progress, and rose to become head of department. He married Jan Harvey (as she was then) in 1965. Both Tom's parents are now dead.

Is there friendship after divorce?

JAN HOWARD

Jan's father was determined that she should acquire some practical training after school which would enable her to earn a living. This was just as well, since she'd been spoiled at home. Her mother Kate was of the old-fashioned opinion that, as Jan was an attractive girl, a husband would soon come along and solve any problems of her having to support herself. Kate has changed her views considerably since then. In fact when she met Tom Jan was just a rather poorly paid assistant in the design department at Southern, a job she'd ended up in after completing the secretarial course her father had insisted she take. In one sense it wasn't until after her divorce that her life really took off.

Their marriage, which took place not long after their meeting, did not entirely please Jan's parents, who'd hoped for someone a little more up-market for their daughter, but as Jan was the apple of their eye they were soon won round and helped finance the young couple's first home. Nevertheless, on Tom's salary Jan had to make do a bit and that irritated her, despite the fact that he worked hard and was clearly capable of better things. Leo was born a year after their marriage, in 1966, and Lynne one year after that. Jan and Tom believed in having children while you were still young enough to enjoy them. Materially, they went from strength to strength: they bought a larger house, a second car and, finally, there was enough spare cash for the *Flying Fish*.

Thus it was that for twenty years or so Jan led an entirely conventional and sheltered life until Tom's redundancy turned her world on its head – and, to her great surprise, turned her into an internationally respected and successful fashion-house chief.

Mother and son

LEO HOWARD Leo has had a tough time. For a long period during and after his parents' break-up, he had to provide a very broad shoulder for people to cry on, but no one wondered if he might need one as well. He gave up university gladly for he was only applying to please his parents, and yet he angered Jan by taking the humble job of pump attendant at a garage. He also had to field for his self-centred sister, Lynne, and to pick up the pieces of the mess Abby Urquhart seemed to be making of her life. It's a wonder he hasn't told the lot of them to get stuffed and gone off to do something on

his own. But marriage to the slinky but dangerous Amanda has taught him
a lot about life, and more about people, and since the divorce proceedings
he has matured more. Still linked in his career to Ken Masters, Leo is now
poised to show himself in his true colours at last, by following a successful
career as a cruiser salesman with one as a power boat racer. But he's
remained true to Abby, and it looks as if she'll get him in the end if she
wants him.

LYNNE HOWARD Lynne is far closer to Tom than Jan. Tom spoils and indulges her, but has also turned her into an expert seawoman. Lynne was very broken up by the sale of the *Flying Fish,* and for a time relations between her and Tom were very strained – something which hurt them both. But had it not been for the loss of her weekend sailing on Tom's boat, she might never have met Jo Penhaligon, never have sailed the Fastnet, and never gained the experience she needed to sail the *Barracuda* single-handed across the Atlantic.

Tom comforts Lynne

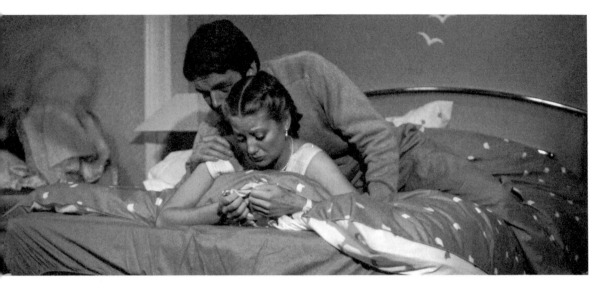

She had a few corners knocked off her by the cynical treatment she received at the hands of Charles Frere. When she ran away from his boat after discovering him in bed with another woman (the lady in question was his American wife, to whom he was fleetingly married, and who only made this one appearance in the serial), she tripped on the jetty, hit her head as she fell into the water, and was nearly drowned. Had it not been for the buoyant quality of salt water she would have died. As it was, she lost her memory, and only recovered it with difficulty. It took great courage for her to prepare and chart her transatlantic voyage, remembering all that Tom had taught her, and then set off in secret, knowing that her father would never have permitted her to go. However, the dangerous journey not only re-established her relationship with Tom, but also taught her far more about herself than she had ever known before. The girl escorted home from America by Claude Dupont, Jan's new French fashion designer, was a girl no longer – she was a woman.

Lynne had still more suffering in store. Her whirlwind romance with Claude, set to end happily in marriage, was shattered when only weeks later he met his tragic death. When we last saw her, Lynne was a more sympathetic, mature person than she had been, and her integrity and courage should bring her all that she wants – one day.

KATE HARVEY

Jan's mother, Kate, who now lives with the family – she had to sell her cottage because of her own financial fecklessness and her weakness for the horses – is quite a sophisticated middle-class English provincial lady, with little time for sentiment and plenty for practical good advice and good deeds. She drives an ancient Morris Traveller dangerously and she is a brilliant gardener and sometimes quite a brilliant gambler too. She knows a horse and has been able to advise Sir Edward Frere on what points to look for in a filly – and she should know, as she had a part share in one once.

Kate with old flame Admiral Redfern – in real life, Dulcie Gray and Michael Denison, the most famous theatrical couple since the Lunts

Her only vice is brandy-and-soda, which is her exclusive alcoholic drink, and she takes it in extreme moderation! She likes Tom if anything more than Jan, and has been more hurt by their break-up than she shows; but she is a fighter and a realist, and without her steadying influence God knows what rocks the Howard clan would have sailed onto.

Kate is a great fighter, with possibly more courage than any of the rest of her family, and it would be nice to think that a romance might bloom for her too. At present the only contenders are Sir Edward Frere and Jack Rolfe, and both men seem to be too interested in chasing after other women! In fact, neither is quite the right man for her. With the brief appearance of Dulcie Gray's real-life husband, Michael Denison, as Admiral Redfern, an old flame and a man worth her salt, there seemed to be an opportunity. However, in real life Michael Denison was too heavily committed to theatre work to continue with the role.

In the meantime, remembering the saying 'unlucky in love, lucky at cards', we can only hope that Kate will make a fortune with her new filly, Spirit of Kate, a gift from Sir Edward, and that she'll recoup the losses which forced her to sell up and move in with her daughter.

KEN MASTERS

It's hard to say who would be front-runner for the villain of the piece, but there's no doubt that Charles Frere and Ken Masters would be vying for first and second places. It's fair to add, though, that neither is an out-and-out baddie. Ken was born in South London in the early forties. He's a shrewd man, totally unscrupulous when need be, and he's got where he has without the benefit of breeding or education. He doesn't have a clue socially though he does his best; and money talks, which helps him, and he has plenty of it. But he's apt to be outclassed and outmanœuvred by

Below left 'Just stay where I can see you.' Will it be a duel to the death between Charles and Ken?
Below right Early days – Ken and Dawn – the downmarket girl he dumps (Sally Farmiloe)

rats to the manner born, such as Sir John Stevens, Sir Edward Frere's pet merchant banker, and nowadays he's venturing onto seas a little deep and a little rough for the kind of boat he's in. He started his working life as a teenage pump attendant at a filling station in Eastleigh near Southampton. With his natural business acumen, he was running the station within six months. Two years later, he owned it. He ended up with a chain of six. The bank was happy, and Ken went on expanding, moving hopefully up market as he bought into the yacht chandlery business. He then acquired Leisurecruise – an ailing power boat company which he reinvigorated despite the tragic suicide of one of his new partners. But Ken isn't the kind of man to let the suicide of a rival bother him for long. Now he's trying to break into 'society', and has already got beyond the women he used to have – tarty blondes – to the women he aspires to: Jan Howard and Sarah Foster. He'll probably start wearing suits more as he gets richer – but it may be a long time before he sheds the identity bracelet and the medallions from round his neck, or learns to wear his signet ring on the proper finger. Ken's still got a long way to go before the Establishment stops raising its eyebrows at him and accepts him.

JACK ROLFE

Jack was born in 1927, and joined the Mermaid Yard as an apprentice twenty years later. He was too young for the war, but did his two years' National Service. Jack's father was a smallholder who prospered for the only time in his life during the war. He saved the money he'd made and, by careful husbandry, managed to make ends meet after the war and until his death. Jack, whose mother had died some years earlier, continued to live at home, but had no wish to follow in his father's footsteps. Even as a kid he'd been fascinated by boats and sailing, and by the time he was in his teens

he had managed to crew for a few retired people, who welcomed a helping hand during wartime when young men were scarce.

Jack proved to be a good apprentice and was kept on at the yard when his apprenticeship was over. Eventually he was made manager by the owner, old Mr Chapman, who was beginning to lose interest. Chapman had married a younger woman after the death of his first wife, and they had a daughter of Jack's age. Jack had all the natural shrewdness associated with good peasant stock, and when Chapman's wife finally left him for a younger and richer man, he consoled the father and daughter and earned their friendship. Jack wanted to be more than manager; he wanted to inherit; and he made sure of that by marrying Eileen.

When Chapman died, he left the yard jointly to his daughter and a long-lost brother of hers, last heard of in New Guinea well over twenty-five years before. Jack felt secure and although the brother did in fact turn up to register a claim (bribed by Charles Frere, who wanted the land the Mermaid stood on for development), the civil action came to nothing. However, Jack, who is long since widowed, carries a burden of guilt that he married Eileen for the yard and not for herself, and that their marriage was an emotionally barren one in which she was miserable. It is the sense of guilt which drives him to drink, as he is a volatile and sentimental man. Nevertheless the marriage was blessed by a daughter, Avril, born in 1957.

Jack has run the yard with a kind of dogged determination, but he has stayed afloat more by luck than judgment, and Tom's appearance on the scene happened in the nick of time.

53

SARAH FOSTER

Sarah, born in 1960, is Ken Masters' latest conquest, though the relationship comes to an end very soon as far as bed is concerned, and becomes strictly business only. She's a slinky blonde Sloane of the type Ken needs to decorate his new image, but she's still too hot for the likes of him to handle properly. She was the brains behind the husband-and-wife team which ran Leisurecruise before Ken stepped in, and she welcomed him for his realistic grasp of business and market trends. Her husband, Mark, a champion power boat racer, was only interested in racing, and when he felt himself outclassed, in the office and in the bedroom, by the new arrival, he ran his boat onto a buoy at top speed in front of Ken and Sarah. But somehow they've manage to live with that. Sarah was very remorseful and guilty initially, since she had no intention of replacing Mark with Ken, and since the suicide Ken has had to tread carefully to keep her sweet and on his side. But Sarah is an unexploded bomb.

SIR EDWARD FRERE

Sir Edward Frere is Jack Rolfe's senior by a few years. We didn't meet him until series three, when he flew in from the British West Indies, where he'd been living in semi-retirement and concentrating on improving his golf. What brought him back to the UK, was news of his son's activities. Convinced that Charles was getting too big for his boots, but also wanting to heal the rift between them so that he would have an heir for his empire, Sir Edward first tried a soft approach. When he was rebuffed by Charles, who could only remember his father as a remote figure, neglectful of him and his mother, Sir Edward decided to 'teach Charles a lesson'.

While part of his mind is on this, another part still desperately seeks an heir. Jan is not too old to have another child, which was principally why he was bent on marrying her; but there remains Abby, his granddaughter, and his great-grandson, William. However, it seems unlikely that Charles Frere would ever let his father's empire fall into any hands but his own.

CHARLES FRERE

Charles was born in the mid-forties. For a long time he was cast as the villain of the piece, but now we are seeing his more human side – the expert rider and the frustrated artist. If only Avril could pierce his armour and get him to relax a little, how much nicer he would be! But he is hell-bent on going one better than his father, and in trying to emulate him he risks becoming just as cold-blooded and just as isolated. Only his artistic French mother's blood redeems him from that fate. Charles is an interesting and at times almost ascetic figure. One can imagine him suddenly throwing his whole empire over and going to live in the South of France to paint.

It is interesting, too, that his one marriage (now over) was occasioned by the necessity to clinch a property deal in the USA. Merciless to his enemies, devious in business practice, at times he appears to be suffering from persecution mania. Yet he is loyal to his friends, though neglectful of them and even churlish to them when they are not in need. He appears to take little pleasure in his wealth, beyond the power it brings him and the ability to buy extraordinarily expensive paintings for Avril. He eats and drinks sparingly, and is a keep-fit fanatic, driving his body as hard as he drives his mind in the business jungle he has chosen to inhabit. The most dangerous thing about Charles, though, is that he could jump any way at all – something which his father does not appear to appreciate. Avril Rolfe seems to be the one steady factor in his life, and their narrow escape from death in the air crash at the end of series three has brought them closer together.

Below left Charles with the suave banker, Sir John Stevens (Willoughby Grey) *Below* Charles sets off for another day's battling in the world of high finance.

AVRIL ROLFE Avril is attractive, efficient, and very self-assured. Jack sent her to boarding school at the age of ten, when her mother died, and it was there that she learned to look after herself. Though she made friends there and was quite popular, she always held part of herself back – a habit she has not yet relinquished.

After school, Avril went on to business college. Jack thought that this would be an excellent training ground for her, with a view to her coming into the boatbuilding business when she graduated and taking over the administration of the Mermaid Yard. The plan was that he would then get

on with the boatbuilding, which he was good at, and the sales, which he sometimes fluffed through drinking too much. Avril, however, had her own ideas. By now she knew her father well, and she knew how he had used her mother. When she completed her business course she told him that she'd been offered a job in London and, despite his protests, she took it and stayed away from home. A few years working in the city gained her valuable experience not only of business but also of people. Avril turned into a thoroughly modern, intelligent, well-dressed, attractive and soph- isticated career-woman. She visited her father occasionally, but never stayed for more than a few days.

It seemed that she was set to carve out a very successful career for herself; then she met Charles. Their original affair was hectic, and lasted a year. She was not inexperienced, but this was her first deep emotional involvement. Then one day Charles left suddenly for the USA on a business trip. A few weeks later she heard that he had married. Deeply shocked as she was, she realised that she'd been wrong in assuming that Charles felt for her as she did for him. Throwing up fresh defences, she returned to Tarrant to help her father, and to bury herself in work very different from that which she'd been doing in London.

Above left Lovers for a time – Avril and Tom
Above Avril

RAISING THE MAST | 59

GERALD URQUHART   Charles Frere's right-hand man is Gerald Urquhart. This quiet and unassuming man is nevertheless a powerful figure in the City and he earns a six-figure salary. Only recently have we learnt the secret he'd been keeping for so long – of his homosexuality. When Gerald's friend, the painter James Gittings, died of AIDS, Charles unexpectedly but perhaps characteristically reimbursed him the £100 000 he'd spent on treatment – an expense which had taken him far into the red and showed the extent and depth of his love. It is hard to see what course the Urquharts' marriage will now take, but so many marriages more or less work as friendly partnerships without sex that there seems no reason for theirs not to.

POLLY URQUHART Gerald's wife, Polly, may not, however, fit so happily into a marriage without sex as her husband. She is too fiery, and too frustrated by her lack of mental stimulation. Bored with her lot, trapped by her money, and not resolute enough to kick over the traces and run, Polly, in her early forties, is suddenly frightened by the speed at which time rushes on towards old age and death. She envies Jan her success but knows that she couldn't follow that road herself; perhaps her main problem is that she doesn't really want to do anything enough to get on and do it.

ABBY URQUHART

Abigail (Abby), their daughter, has, at twenty-two, sorted her life out better than either of her parents. She has survived a suicide attempt, an affair with a pathological animal rights activist, a pregnancy, and a failed marriage. She has returned from the States with a clear idea of what she wants to do – photography – and with all the poise and self-assurance her mother used to long for her to have, and which she failed to acquire at finishing school. When Leo sees her again he is sure of what he has always inwardly felt – that she was the one for him, right from the start. But she has been away and seen the world, while he has stayed at home. Will they still have enough in common, or will they have grown apart?

Below Admiring grandparents – though the baby's arrival is a mixed blessing

Will they, won't they?
Leo and Abby

Right Where it all began – Tom Howard, flanked by his children Leo and Lynne, aboard the *Flying Fish*, the first boat Tom designed

Not all the characters were fully drawn right from the outset, and as we will see, it took careful casting and intelligent acting to put flesh and blood on the bones constructed in the early script conferences and creative-planning meetings. An interesting aspect of characters created for a drama like *Howards' Way*, which has no actual ending, is that it mirrors life very closely. An actor confronted with a part like Hamlet knows exactly what happens to the character and how he ends up, and can approach his role armed with that knowledge. It is very difficult to play a character whose ultimate fate has not been determined and who, in the future, may show traits of character still unknown to anyone. *Howards' Way* has a large number of 'main' characters, and directors, designers and even writers come and go. Thus it is that the actor is the only true custodian of his own character. The actors and the producer provide the one constant thread right through all the series, and so from the very first casting had to be spot-on. The trials and tribulations of this task are what we look at next.

Right Once the *Flying Fish* had been sold to raise money for Tom to buy into the Mermaid Yard, Lynne had to find crewing work wherever she could get it. Here she is with Phil Norton (Anthony Head) aboard his boat the *Mickey Mouse*

Opposite page
Top Is this the boat that launched a thousand deals? Charles Frere aboard his luxury motor cruiser
Below left Tony Anholt plays Charles Frere, captain of industry
Below right Sail on! The £500 000-cruiser epitomises Charles's wealth and power

poetry in motion – Barracuda

pposite page
ain photograph All aboard. A crowded
arracuda of Tarrant shows not only the
*ctors, but the film crew and the profes-
*onal sailing crew, who we don't see on
ur screens
sets left Avril Rolfe launches the *Barra-
cuda and Tom and Leo put her through her
aces
sets right A commercially-marketed
*arracuda moored among other boats
*a preparation for the start of the Single-
*anded Transatlantic Yacht Race,
*ymouth 1988 and *(below) Barracuda*
*veeps past admiring crowds before the
art of the same race

Left Leo checks the stays aboard
one of his father's latest creations
– *Spring of Tarrant*
Top The snug interior of *Spring*
Above Hi there! Edward Highmore,
who plays Leo, wouldn't mind a
Spring of his own

Opposite page Mark Foster
(Graham Poutney) aboard his
Cougar power boat and *(inset)*
Ready for the off! Mark prepares
to race

CHAPTER THREE

Recruiting the Crew

~~~

Actors face a quandary when they are cast in long-running television dramas. There is always the fear of being type-cast, but against that is the attraction of being very much in the public eye and of earning steady and (by the standards of the theatre) generous money. There are also fringe benefits: a popular television actor or actress can earn around £2000 for one personal appearance.

They earn their living. The cast of *Howards' Way* is involved with the show throughout the production year, from February until October, and during that time there is little or no opportunity to do anything else. In the winter breaks, some of them have taken pantomime work – something which Glyn Owen, who plays Jack Rolfe, particularly enjoys – but otherwise they are more or less continuously committed to the serial.

Many of the actors have had to learn to sail. Their teacher is Bob Fisher, involved since the beginning as sailing consultant. He has taught the crew at least the rudiments of sailing. Tracey Childs became very good. Maurice Colbourne, Glyn Owen and Edward Highmore have also become more expert through frequent sailing, but during film sequences on board Bob and an expert skeleton crew are there, off camera, and have real control of the boat. That isn't so bad on a big yacht like *Barracuda*, but it's a tight squeeze on *Spring* – especially since the director and camera crew are on board as well.

Stand-ins are almost never used, and stuntmen rarely. A stunt girl was used when Lynne (Tracey) fell off the walkway into the water at the

Left Poetry in motion – Take 2! Inspired by the series, *Spring* is the most commercially successful yacht ever, says her real-life designer Tony Castro

Right Under sail.
Barracuda

Top left Tom at the
mooring
Above Jack's a great
yachtsman, too . . .

end of series two, but when the sequence was shot, in the usual British pouring rain, Tracey herself slipped and fell in. Stuntmen were used for Mark Foster's suicide, Richard Spencer's power boat accident, Claude Dupont's death, and Richard Shellet's murder attempt on Jack. In this last sequence, they bought an old boat to blow up, but the special-effects people controlled the explosion so carefully that damage to the boat was minimal. It was subsequently sold and is now back sailing.

Once the series was under way, the actors in the main roles took on the characters for themselves, and brought much of themselves to their fictional counterparts. In consequence, the writers began to write for the character given flesh and blood by the actor. It's always easier when you are writing drama of this sort to know what the character looks like, and new writing recruits are encouraged to watch videos of past episodes to get the feel of the people and the 'house style'. Because writers and directors may change from series to series, the actors become the custodians of their characters, knowing, if you like, what is best for them. They may even have suggestions for their character's storyline, but, since they tend to see the whole show from their character's point of view, such suggestions are carefully vetted!

Keeping the actors is always a source of uncertainty. After the first two series, their agents would allow them to be booked only one series ahead (which is standard practice) and in any case the entire team knows only one series ahead if they are to continue at all. Once *Howards' Way* had established itself as a roaring success, the actors wanted more money. They got a large rise for series three but, budgets being what they are, only the usual percentage rise for series four, the one broadcast in autumn 1988. So far, nobody has jibbed at this.

There is never any ill-feeling about people wanting to leave the cast. Cindy Shelley, who plays Abby, wanted some time out to go back to the theatre, since she had done nothing but television for some time – *Tenko* followed by two years of *Howards' Way*. That was fine, and they were equally happy to see her back when she wanted to return. Her absence even provided a good storyline, since the character could be sent to the USA and develop 'off-stage'.

There was no problem with the early casting. Gerry is not keen on auditioning and prefers to cast on the basis of conversations about the roles with actors whom he's either worked with before or whose work he knows. 'Auditions can give a false impression. You may get a brilliant one from an actor who then makes no further progress; alternatively a good actor may fail an audition simply because nerves make him spoil his chances.' He also tries hard to avoid casting to type and will never, for example, cast as a lawyer an actor who is always seen playing lawyers – he might cast such an actor as a bus driver. He knew exactly whom he wanted to play Jack, Ken and Kate: he had worked with Glyn Owen on *The Brothers*, and with Stephen Yardley and Dulcie Gray before too. He'd seen Tony Anholt's work (Charles) and he'd watched Susan Gilmore (Avril) play a mad Norwegian in a TV thriller.

A problem arose with Tom. The great difficulty in casting, especially for film and television, is to find actors who look believable. It's not just a question of a good performer; you must find someone who looks as if he might be interested in boats, as if he could be a boatbuilder, and who looks right when you put him on a boat. Not many British actors share the

rugged, outdoor quality which many Australian and American actors have. Gerry remembers a remark made by an American colleague: 'You've got a lot of great actors over here, but most of them only look OK in a drawing-room.' When Gerry saw Maurice Colbourne, he knew he'd found the right man.

No one who works on *Howards' Way* see it as just another job; everyone enjoys it and wants to make their contributions count. That this is so is very much down to Gerry, who is always accessible and makes everyone feel involved. One of the keys to any successful venture is team spirit, and Gerry's method of achieving this is not to employ stars. The aim is to cast good professional actors and, with the success of the series, to

make them stars. Because of the way filming and studio work is scheduled, not all the actors meet each other all the time, but there is a great sense of ensemble among them. At the end of every series, they have an 'end-of-term' party, which usually includes a cabaret, to which Jonathan Powell insists on being invited.

The parties are usually organised by Jan Harvey and Stephen Yardley. The first was held at Henrietta's, the Putney restaurant run by Ivor Danvers' wife. Jonathan Powell hosted a spoof Oscar ceremony for the most interesting contributions to *Howards' Way* over the year. The 'Oscars' were plastic potted cacti. The third party featured an 'Episode Fourteen', written by Stephen Yardley and Edward Highmore, which sent up the scripts: 'Everyone's always suggesting lunch or dinner, and off-screen characters like Lynne are constantly sending letters to remind us all that they're still alive!'

The camaraderie is the seal of a really happy show.

CHAPTER FOUR

The Crew

~~~

The main characters in *Howards' Way* must have some of the best-known faces in Britain at the moment. The series is also seen in Holland and Belgium, Norway and Switzerland, Hong Kong, New Zealand and Australia, where it's such a smash hit that Aussies here on holiday have been agog to see members of the cast in the street. Now, of course, there's an Australian character, Mike Hanley. What are these people like off-screen? And what do they think of the characters they play?

JAN HARVEY

'It's a wig this year — or anyway, a half-wig.' Jan Harvey was referring to Jan Howard's famous hair-do, more copied even than Princess Di's. Her own hairstyle is much softer, and reflects a personality which is essentially different from that of her namesake. 'It makes me just a little bit more difficult to recognise, I hope. Anyway I prefer my hair this way.'

The first thing about her that strikes you, apart from her beauty and charm and the length of her legs, is her warmth. She was born in Redruth in 1947, the daughter of a garage proprietor and a teacher, and moved to Penzance when she was three years old. Both her parents were Cornish born and bred, and had met through local amateur operatic societies, in which her mother was a leading light. Even if Jan was the first of her family to go into the theatre professionally, she already had it in her blood. Her original ambition, though, was to follow her mother (and several of her other maternal relatives) into teaching. Despite an early education which included ballet school ('I did all the exams') and teenage appearances at the famous Minack Theatre, she went to Homerton Teacher Training College at Cambridge to take a B.Ed. 'I remember when I went up there for my interview. I was a real country hick, and I was bowled over by the place, it was so beautiful. I think the most wonderful moment of my life was when the postman came with my letter of acceptance. I only read the first few words: "We are pleased to . . ." I threw the letter up in the air and danced down the road in sheer joy — it was only when I got to the corner that I realised the letter might have gone on: ". . . have seen you at the interview but we are sorry we can't offer you a place." So I had to dash back and read the rest of it.'

One of her teachers at school had advised her to get straight into Cambridge University theatre but, like so many people before and since, when she was confronted by the gurus of the Amateur Dramatic Club, the Footlights and the Marlowe Society, she was so daunted that she fled and didn't act for the whole of her first year. Later on, as a joke, a friend put her name down for an audition without her knowledge; she went along and got the part. Later that year she played Desdemona in Shakespeare's *Othello* in the Queens' College summer production, and rediscovered her taste for the stage. 'I did an audition for Footlights [the cradle of Peter Cook and Jonathan Miller] at about the same time. It must have been the worst audition they'd ever heard. My accompanist, through no fault of his own, had to play an octave higher than we'd rehearsed, so I practically had to speak my song. I was being auditioned by Germaine Greer and Clive James. She said, "Christ, the girl can't sing." He said: "She stayed on stage though — that's more than most people would have done!" '

She got into the Marlowe Society and her crowning achievement was playing Ophelia in *Hamlet*. Shortly afterwards, she married the play's director, Kerry Crabbe, but although he went into the theatre professionally she didn't – 'I thought one of us in that business is quite enough.' In any case, it had not occurred to her that acting was something one might actually do for a living.

She went into teaching, and enjoyed her two years at infant schools in London; but she spent her spare time studying theatre, and with the break-up of her marriage (they remain friends) she decided to try it professionally. 'I made a kind of half-step first, and went to do Theatre-in-Education at York. It was hard work, but very rewarding. I played everything from brigands to centurions, and once a witch called Catastrophe.' When she was playing the witch, she had a moving experience. During a performance at a special school she asked one of the little girls in the audience a question – and got a reply. 'I noticed a sort of *frisson* among the teachers nearby, but I didn't think anything of it until after the play was over. Then a teacher came up to me and said, "Do you know, that little girl has never spoken before?" It just shows how powerful drama can be, and it was a great feeling, though of course it was really nothing to do with me.'

After nine months in York she was ready to try straight theatre, and returned to London. Her first part was as a sprite in a production of *The Tempest*, but her West End début marked the real beginning of her career. 'I played Mrs Duck in *Toad of Toad Hall*. My first lines on the West End stage were "Quack, quack!" And I had to lay an egg in the courtroom scene. That used to bring the house down. I doubled as a ferret in that production, and I remember when my parents came to see the show my father was worried that he wouldn't be able to work out which ferret I was under the make-up. I told him not to worry, and when I came on stage I wore his deerstalker!'

Television beckoned soon after, and since the early seventies she has played a number of character roles, notably in *Sam*, *A Family Affair* and *Fell Tiger*, the series she made immediately before *Howards' Way*. 'One thing that's plagued me recently is having the same name as my character. In *Fell Tiger* I played someone called Susan Harvey, and in this it's even closer: Jan Howard's maiden name is Harvey! The worst thing, though, is the same Christian name. That can be a bit of a bugbear. In a restaurant, someone

Jan as she appeared in *A Family Affair* in 1979 (as Susan West)

will suddenly call out, "Jan!" I'm a bit short-sighted and by the time I've responded and focused on whoever it is I realise that it's not a friend but someone who knows me from *Howards' Way*. It's easier for the others in that way. If someone hails Maurice Colbourne as "Tom", he knows immediately that there's a programme connection.'

She thinks herself lucky not to have been type-cast, and feels it may have something to do with having a chameleon-like character. 'I can change the way I look very easily, which probably means that I'll never be a big, recognisable star; but I'm not complaining!' She's always rather liked Jan Howard, whom she sees as a tough, abrasive woman who has always been positive and known where she's going. 'She never really was the little woman, though she probably fell into that role for a long time because it was what Tom wanted. I admire her for realising that at forty she still had at least twenty years of working life left to fulfil her ambitions; and I have to hand it to Gerry for creating that kind of character. I know that there are many women who are in exactly Jan Howard's position. Although I don't have children myself, I can well imagine the difficulties in developing your ambitions and looking after the family you've created.' Her ambitions and her interests are wide. 'I'd like to travel more, and professionally there are many areas to explore. I'm writing a sitcom at the moment, and one day I'd like to do some production. The only thing I've never wanted to do, oddly, is direct.' As far as acting is concerned, she would like the chance to work in plays by Chekhov, Ibsen and Strindberg.

Her taste is nothing like Jan Howard's, and she has no difficulty at all in seeing where Jan Howard ends and Jan Harvey begins. 'Probably the only thing we have absolutely in common is our car; we both drive the same model, an Isuzu Piazza Turbo. Otherwise, I think that if Jan Howard and I met at a dinner party I'd have nothing to say to her; I'd probably find her too blinkered and self-assured. But I like to think that if I bothered to make friends with her I'd be pleasantly surprised.' In real life she would never wear the same clothes as her character. She rehearses in a sweater and jeans, but puts on high heels for the Producer's Run (roughly the TV equivalent of a full rehearsal) to work her way into the character. She enjoys wearing clothes by Roland Klein, Lanvin, Yves St Laurent and Yuki,

but she enjoys them as costumes – a means to portraying the character. 'In real life I couldn't afford them, for a start; but in any case I wouldn't wear them. I like to feel relaxed in the clothes I wear.' The character goes on with the make-up, the hair-do, and the frocks. 'One of the people who was really pleased when I got the part was my mother. She thought I might start dressing more like Jan, but she was disappointed.'

Although she dislikes shopping, she is careful about Jan Howard's wardrobe and shops with the costume designer. It has been a revelation to explore the world of *haute couture*. 'Jan Howard's image is part of her job, so when I go shopping on her behalf I can be quite picky!' At the end of each series the artists are able to buy the clothes bought for their characters at a discount, and she has done so occasionally, but even so the clothes are pretty pricey. 'It depends, too, on which designer's clothes we're using, because we change from series to series, and the costume designers change too, and have different favourites. So we mix and match. I love the Italian designers, like Armani, but they're prohibitively expensive here,

more than they cost in New York.' In private life, Jan Howard's style has affected her only in so far as she dresses the part for personal appearances. She has opened boat shows and boutiques and been involved with charities like Children in Need and the RNLI Appeal. 'But it's difficult. When you're well known, you get so many requests for help, and you just can't help everybody.'

Unlike Jan Howard, Jan Harvey has developed a taste for sailing. It began when she was asked to take part in the Round the Island race on the trimaran *Red Star* in 1986. 'We bucketed round the Isle of Wight on a miserable day and I loved every minute of it. The thing about sailing is that it gives you time to be alone with yourself. I am a very gregarious person and I think sometimes that I don't give myself enough time like that; but so far I haven't taken up sailing too seriously.' Her hobbies, when she has time for them, are decorating and gardening. 'It probably sounds really dull, but I *love* gardening. I only wish I had more room, but you don't get acres of space in Battersea! Still, I've got hibiscus and rhododendrons and clematis … I even take my morning cup of coffee out to the garden sometimes and have a chat with my plants.' She enjoys eating out too, but does so less now that she tends to be recognised; though she has never found people less than polite. 'On the whole, people seem to like the character of Jan; many of the letters that come in are from women, some even asking me to sign birthday cards to their husbands!' Compensating for not going out to eat, she likes entertaining at home, or just having a glass of white burgundy with friends. And she is interested in everything. She may be a far cry from Jan Howard, but they do have two things in common: liveliness and spirit.

MAURICE COLBOURNE

Maurice Colbourne plays Tom Howard. His original ambition was to run away to sea – the result, he thinks, of not wanting to go into the steel business and of reading too much Marryat and Conrad when he was a boy. He tried it, though he arrived in Liverpool from his native Sheffield to find the town in the middle of a slump, and ranks of seamen queueing for the dole. 'So that nipped my career in the Merchant Navy in the bud.'

He'd broken an apprenticeship to a stonemason in Sheffield, so he didn't feel there was any turning back. He made his way to Manchester and got a job as a fairground roustabout, working on the ghost train at Bellevue, and then spent several months on the travelling fairs. They were pretty demoralising, 'though there were some amazing characters; I remember the wife of the director of one fair – she could lay out a man with a single blow.' He ended up in London. 'I was in my early twenties. What I wanted to do was become a writer, but I had no idea how to go about it. I got a job as a waiter to keep body and soul together. One day one of the other waiters asked a friend to take over his shift, as he was doing a film part in *The Loneliness of the Long-Distance Runner*, and I remember that some time afterwards Tom Courtenay, who played the lead in it, came in to have a chat with him.'

He soon had the idea of becoming an actor himself, and this was reinforced by the renaissance the theatre was going through at the time. 'Also, it was one of the few careers open to a man like me, since you could do it without any qualifications.' After a couple of false starts, he auditioned for the Central School of Speech and Drama and got a place. Three years later he emerged as a qualified actor and went into repertory theatre, in Leicester, Birmingham, and then Leicester again, leading the nomadic life of all young actors. 'There was a great repertoire in those days. We were doing Shakespeare one week and Brecht the next, but we wanted to do

Below Maurice in the role that brought him fame – John Kline in the unforgettable *Gangsters* (BBC tv, 1977)

more experimental stuff too.' At the end of the sixties he joined a new theatre touring group founded by playwright David Hare, and became involved in Jim Haines's Arts Lab. For a long time, Maurice worked in experimental and fringe theatre, which culminated in his becoming a director of the Half Moon Theatre in the East End of London. It was housed in a defunct synagogue: 'I lived on one of the balconies there for a time, and another actor lived on the other balcony with his wife, his two kids and a red setter!'

The move to television came in the mid-seventies with the lead in the controversial BBC series, *Gangsters*. 'The opportunity came at precisely the right moment, though at first I was in two minds. Although by now I was an honorary Cockney, having lived in the East End for so long, I felt we were doing too many plays set in the area, which put me at odds with the other directors at the Half Moon.' Television has brought rewards and

problems: 'I carry a wad of *Howards' Way* scripts and papers around with me so that I can keep track of where we are, because we do the scenes very much out of order. The techniques of acting are very different from those you use on stage.' The character of Tom is also a departure for him: 'Usually I get cast as a villain, which I have to say I quite enjoy playing.'

He'd done some sailing before *Howards' Way*, though he remembers a disastrous trip he made once with a couple of fishermen out of Barbados. 'I was as sick as a dog. The boat was tiny and the waves were mountainous, and on top of that there was the smell of the petrol from the engine and the smell of the fish they were cutting up as bait for the sharks.' No such problems have beset him on *Howards' Way* and it has made him a keen sailor. 'There's no doubt that sailing is the coming thing; I can foresee far more sailing holidays and boat chartering in the future.' Unlike Tom, he prefers wood to glass fibre, but hasn't yet made any plans to buy a boat. He doesn't drive the same kind of car either. Tom has a Jaguar; Maurice has a Volvo 480ES. 'I have to do a hell of a lot of travelling, between London, Southampton and Birmingham, and we need a big car when the whole family's aboard – wife, daughter and cats.' There are three cats, and the marmalade one, Albie, insists on going on location.

Maurice met his wife on Hampstead Heath: 'She was jogging, and I was fishing.' Chan Lian Si, or Jeany as she's also called, is a Malay Chinese, and was working as a nurse when they met. Their daughter, Clara, was born in 1980. 'Jeany speaks Mandarin Chinese, Hokien Chinese, and Malay – which is a very interesting language – but fortunately for me she was also brought up speaking English.' For the past few years he and his family have led a nomadic life, first moving back to Sheffield, then to London again, through a succession of flats and houses, so until recently he hasn't had much time to pursue his interests.

'I love sixties pop – anything from The Beatles to Crosby, Stills, Nash and Young – but it's only recently that we've been able to unpack the sound system.' His favourite reading is biography (recently, Richard Ellman's work on Oscar Wilde), 'and I've been reading Samuel Butler's *The Way of All Flesh*, which really is a revelation.' Another hobby is fishing, which he keeps up on the large reservoirs just to the north of his home in

Hackney. 'In summer, I leave the rehearsal rooms in Acton, travel home on the hot and dusty tube, pick up some sandwiches and a flask, or maybe a can of Special Brew, bung my rugs in the car, and within ten minutes I can be on the bankside, casting my eyes around for fish.' He likes horse-racing, especially National Hunt. 'I'd love to own a horse, and it'd be a great idea if *Howards' Way* had one running, but of the entire cast only Nigel Davenport and Dulcie Gray really share my interest.' Still on the gambling side, he likes the occasional game of poker, 'but I'm far from being a second Nathan Detroit'.

Maurice doesn't admit to being a countryman at heart, but there is clearly a great love of the country in him. At one stage he and his wife considered opening a Malaysian restaurant in Bristol, but when they shelved the idea an alternative was to move to Hampshire and take over a mushroom farm. 'It's a beautiful part of the world, and the people are relaxed and tolerant. We'd taken it as far as arranging a loan from the bank, and everything was ready to roll, but at the last minute we re-checked the figures and found that we'd be working more for the bank than ourselves. I wouldn't want to live in the country without working there. I haven't much time for weekend-cottage types.'

A lot of his time is taken up replying to fan mail. He answers every letter, though the volume is such that he doesn't have time, to his regret, to hand-write every one. Many are from younger girls – 'surprisingly,' he adds modestly. Other letters request items for charity auctions. 'I'm a keen trout fisherman, and I once had a letter asking me if I had any unwanted tackle to donate to an angling club for the disabled, so I tied them some flies. But I don't get any letters suggesting anything . . . how shall I say . . . intriguing!'

Maurice has a distinctive face and is no stranger to being greeted in public. Most of the time people are friendly, 'but you can get some very strange reactions. I remember once I'd taken the train to Sheffield and when we arrived I went to fetch my bicycle from the baggage car. The porter was outraged: "You're that Maurice Colbourne, aren't you?" he said. "Where's your bloody Rolls–Royce?"' Some people think that all actors live their lives on the Burton–Taylor level.

As Tom is a designer, Maurice thinks that he would always have a certain sense of style, but that his priorities would be his boat and his car not his clothes. 'He would care about what he wears, but his choice is dictated by his job. His predominant colour is blue.' Maurice is not a man whose first consideration is clothes, but he admits to a greater interest in them since he began work on the serial; and inevitably there's a public image to live up to which is a far cry from the old Arts Lab days. 'And your taste in clothes and even your dress sense is developed when you go out shopping with the costume designer. Apart from that, old Tom's got to hold his own if he's playing a scene with Avril or Jan, both dressed like a million dollars!'

EDWARD HIGHMORE

Edward Highmore (Leo Howard), was born in Kingston-upon-Thames, the son of an accountant, and now lives in a flat in north London. Like Maurice, he did not set out to be an actor. 'I wanted to be a tree surgeon, and I went to agricultural college at Merrist Wood to train; but I wasn't very good at chemistry, and so they slung me out, which meant I had to think again.'

He'd done some drama at school and enjoyed it; so decided to try his luck professionally, but at the Guildford School of Acting he first trained as a dancer. Leo is not his first part in television. He has appeared in *Tripods*, *Doctor Who* and *Lame Ducks*. He also recently played Frank in *Mrs Warren's Profession* at the Leeds Playhouse. In a short career, he admits to having been very lucky. 'There's been plenty of work and very little unemployment. I'd say that my ambition would be to keep things that way.' He got the role of Leo after one of the directors on *Howards' Way* had worked with him at the Actors' Centre in London. 'A lot of people thought that Leo was rather a drip at first, but I think they lost sight of the fact that he was very young – pretty well the youngest character – and we've tried to show him growing up and becoming more self-assured.'

Leo was saddled with the role of knight in shining armour at one stage because he was shoring up Abby, his sister Lynne, and even his mother, Jan, during the break-up of her marriage. Edward thinks that the image of goody-goody was one the press latched on to: 'It's easy for them to label people; Leo became that sort of person, full stop, just as Ken became Mr Wicked.' He would like to see Leo climb out from under the weight of other people's problems, and it looks as if his wishes are coming true, as he moves from success as a power boat salesman to being a power boat racer. He's sure, too, that Leo's made progress because his fan mail's changed; instead of letters from very young girls, he now finds that he's getting a lot from people of his own age. There are still some who write to Leo asking for advice or giving it, and he got plenty warning him off Amanda!

Now that Leo has moved out of jeans and into suits, his taste and Edward's have parted company. 'I find that as the year progresses, I get scruffier and scruffier as a kind of antidote to wearing all those trendy suits and having to worry about keeping the creases sharp!' His car, too, is a straightforward VW Golf. 'Leo's Panther Callista is a lovely car, a wonderful car, but it's not exactly practical. You'd need a second car to do the shopping, in real life!'

He had never been sailing before *Howards' Way*, but now finds that he really enjoys it, and might even take it up one day if he has the time and the money. 'But my main pastime is conversation, and what I enjoy most is being with my friends and going out to dinner or the theatre with my girlfriend.' He gives the impression of a man who is content with his lot.

DULCIE GRAY

Dulcie Gray, who plays Jan's mother, Kate Harvey, has done no fewer than 107 plays, and just about half of them were with her husband Michael Denison, who appeared briefly in *Howards' Way* as Admiral Redfern. Her first-ever acting job was opposite him, in Aberdeen. 'We met and became engaged at drama school, but he graduated before me. When he was offered a job in Scotland, I was finishing school, but he didn't want to leave me behind. Luckily the play's director had seen me in the end-of-term productions and liked me, so he gave me a job too. We got married in London on a Saturday morning, and then Michael had to do a final matinée and evening performance at the Westminster Theatre while I packed our bags for Scotland. We had one night's honeymoon, travelled to Aberdeen on the Sunday, and began work on Monday morning.' They celebrate their fiftieth wedding anniversary – and fifty years in the theatre – in 1989.

Dulcie's first job had nothing to do with the theatre. She was a schoolteacher at Fraser's Hill in the Malayan jungle. The daughter of a lawyer, she was born in Kuala Lumpur, but returned to England at the age of three when her parents came back on leave. 'All the children used to come home quite early in those days because of the climate.' Her parents returned to Malaya without her, and she did not see them again until she was eight. 'But I went to a boarding school in Wallingford, where I was really very happy.' She returned to Malaya when she was fourteen, but home life was unhappy and she ran away. At sixteen she had begun to teach, and was soon contributing a gossip column to *The Straits Tribune*. 'I was earning five shillings a week for a twelve-hour day; I had to augment my income somehow.' The paper paid her three times as much for her weekly 'Fraser's Hill Notes' as she was paid for teaching.

She also wrote songs, one or two of which she's revived at the

Howards' Way end-of-series parties. One has the immortal title of 'You Tickle Me Spitless, Baby, I'm Just Wild About You'! She learnt Malay and still speaks it fluently, but she didn't find enough to amuse her in Malaya and wanted to return to England. She managed to get a job accompanying a child of two back on a cargo boat: 'I arrived here with £10 in my pocket, but I was seventeen and a half, and full of hope.' A job as games mistress at her old school fell through when she broke her arm. She lived with her uncle, Cyril Bailey, then Public Orator at Oxford University, but won a scholarship studying art with the surrealist, Amédée Ozenfant. 'My mother was a painter and I think she always wanted me to become one; but I never felt tempted to follow that path, though the smell of oil paint still gives me a shiver of pleasure. I don't think I was good enough to be a professional painter, anyway, and now I don't even paint as a hobby.'

'While I was on the painting scholarship I was living in a tiny room in London and starving, really starving; one had splitting headaches and stomach cramps. I used to go to art galleries to keep warm, but it was a wonderful time. Epstein used to give huge high teas for students – he knew what it was like to be poor. In those days one could buy one of his paintings for £60. It was way out of my reach, but I still can't help thinking, "If only …!"' She likes the very early Italians, like Mantegna and Fra Lippo Lippi, the Impressionists and Modigliani. Though she met Braque, Chagall and Léger, she has never really liked 'modern' art. 'With one or two exceptions, I stop around 1900!'

A career in the theatre came about by chance. When the scholarship with Ozenfant came to an end, she had to find some new source of income, not wanting to pursue painting as a career. She found there was a scholarship being offered by the Webber Douglas Academy of Dramatic Art, went in for it and won it. Things simply went on from there.

Dulcie does have a second career, however – writing. Some years ago owing to the misdiagnosis of a serious illness, she was told that she had eight months to live. 'I didn't tell Michael, which was foolish; and not unnaturally I couldn't sleep, so I used to go downstairs and write; it seemed the quietest thing to do.' She has now published twenty-two books, including thrillers and novels, and is working on a novel set in Kenya. 'I always start with the place, and then the characters sort of grow out of it, but I like to know where I am to begin with.'

She is also a naturalist and is particularly interested in insects. Her study of British butterflies, *Butterflies On My Mind*, published by Angus and Robertson in 1978, won *The Times Educational Supplement* Senior Information Award. British butterflies and their conservation are her major interest, and not surprisingly that book is among her favourites. 'But I also like some of my more horrendous books, like *Babyface* and *Murder in Mind*.' She admires Rebecca West, who was a personal friend, Anthony Powell, Dickens, Scott, Jane Austen and the Brontës.

She has tried to bring much of her own experience of life to Kate Harvey. 'I think Kate probably lived overseas for a long time when her husband was alive. She's very broad-minded and independent in spirit, but I am glad she likes horse-racing and gardening, as I do, though I have to admit that Michael does most of the gardening. It's splendid that she's been given a job, too, and I think working in the boutique has done Kate a lot of good. It's got her out of the kitchen and into some much better clothes; her original scene was wellies and a battered gardening hat.' Kate's personality and manner are very clear in her mind, and, in common with all the actors, she keeps a close eye on how her character is treated. The BBC rotate costume designers on and off the show, and new ones may not be familiar with the character or have a clear idea of what clothes are right. Dulcie sees that they do.

Fan mail comes in from viewers of all types and ages, but especially from people who are a little down in the dumps, who write to Kate for some of the sound, positive advice for which she is so well known. *Howards' Way* has developed quite a cult following among the young too, and Kate gets a number of appreciative letters from teenagers.

Like Kate, Dulcie loves the countryside and lives in it. 'We've always had dogs too, and it's nicer for them out of town.' Their first dog was a corgi, who appeared in five films. Then followed 'thirty years of labradors'. Now they have a corgi again, named Brett. 'It wasn't the name we'd have chosen, but he came to us when he was eight months old, and by then he'd learnt it and it was too late to change it.' Dulcie and her husband

Dulcie as Barbara Hale in the 1964 television production of *East Lynne*

live in an eighteenth-century house. 'The eighteenth century really is *my* century. I love the architecture and the art of that time, and although it was a century like ours in some ways they spent their money on beauty. I get depressed by the lack of beauty in our environment, especially in architecture, and I believe it is bad for people to be surrounded by ugly things and to live in ugly buildings.' Kate Harvey would certainly agree.

STEPHEN YARDLEY

A Yorkshireman by birth, Stephen Yardley (wheeling and dealing Ken Masters) was raised in Essex and went to Brentwood School. It's a public school and although Stephen doesn't speak with a public school accent, he's a long way from the Cockney businessman he portrays.

He didn't like school much, because he had a terrible stutter 'and, kids being kids, my classmates used to love taking the piss out of me.' When he left, his father, who worked for Norwich Union, encouraged him to work in marine insurance in the City. 'I hated it, but I stuck it for about a year, and then I just had to find something else.' He took a job on a building site and quickly worked his way up to being a superhod, which means that he was hod-carrying for two brickies simultaneously. 'I knew that wasn't the limit of my ambition, though!' In the meantime, he was training himself out of his stutter, a social hang-up he couldn't stand.

One day in the library he picked up a copy of *The Stage*, the theatrical trade paper, and noticed an advertisement from Richmond Theatre for a student Assistant Stage Manager – about the lowliest theatre job there is and the one in which most people start. 'They were offering £1 a week, and I thought it quite ridiculous. I was earning £35 a week hod-carrying

Stephen played parti-
san Max Brocard in
Gerard Glaister's
Secret Army series
in 1978

and in those days, the late fifties, that was riches. Beer was a shilling a pint, and I bought my first car for £4.' Nevertheless, he decided to go for the job. He was intrigued, apart from anything else. He got it and worked as a student ASM for three months, 'then they promoted me to ASM and my wages went up to a fiver.'

He was hooked. Still on the stage management side, as he was able to read music he went to work at the Royal Opera House, and then on the première, at Aldeburgh, of Benjamin Britten's *A Midsummer Night's Dream*. Then more repertory at Colchester and Westcliffe, and a successful audition for the Royal Academy of Dramatic Art, where he studied from 1960 to 1963. At the end of his course the principal, John Fernald, said: 'I don't know how you're going to get on in the business ... maybe you'll get the occasional part in a Pinter play, who knows?' 'I don't think he was trying to be encouraging,' says Stephen, 'but I thought the occasional Pinter play would suit me down to the ground, and I have in fact played Deeley in *Old Times* at the Liverpool Playhouse.'

He's played a great variety of roles, including many from Shakespeare. 'I think at one time and another I've done practically all the Mechanicals in *A Midsummer Night's Dream*.' But his favourite part of all was Bosola in *The Duchess of Malfi*, which he did for Theatr Clwyd. He'd like to play Iago, 'and I'd like to have another go at Cassius and Astrov in Chekhov's *Uncle Vanya*.' Of his many television parts, the ones he remembers with greatest pleasure are *The XYY Man*, and the Russian pianist in *Secret Army*.

'When I came to the part of Ken, he was pretty well worked out as a character. I'd played that kind of working-class London boy a couple of times before, which is probably why they thought of me, and I wanted to develop the character a little further. I remember that I was having a week's holiday in Spain with a friend, and I wanted to have a look at Benidorm, which really does have to be seen to be believed. We wandered into a bar, and there was this guy who *was* Ken – everything was perfect: the white leather jacket, the medallions, even the "gold sovereign" rings. I drew the line at the rings, but I borrowed a good deal of the rest of his style. Then later I had the idea of wearing sweaters without shirts underneath – it's the kind of thing Ken would think cool – and we got splendid letters saying things like, "It's too revolting for words", so I knew I'd got it right!'

Ken's wardrobe is carefully worked out. His clothes are bought in Austin Reed, Cecil Gee, and Harrods; his suits are made by Henry Rose of Savile Row, and his shirts are made specially too. 'I've got three suits for Ken and they are really fabulous. I'd buy them myself if I could afford them.' The trick is getting very expensive clothes and mis-matching them. 'And the costume designer and I always go for light shades and pastel colours to contrast with the dark clothes the other blokes wear. That's part of the fantasy of *Howards' Way*, really; summer really is summer, and the characters go around in boats dressed elegantly and lightly, not like real life where they're wrapped up in macs against the wind and the driving rain.'

Ken has done well for himself but has missed out on the kind of education which teaches that class goes with understatement. He's also very vain. 'He wears all the gold jewellery to show off how well he's done, and that is quite true to life.' Stephen, sitting outside the studio in Birmingham, is in costume. He toys with the huge gold identity bracelet on his wrist, with 'Ken' engraved on it in copperplate. 'I think Dawn probably gave Ken that,' he jokes. Dawn, the little blonde Ken was shacked up with in the first series, was the only girl we've seen him with of his own class. Otherwise, with Jan and especially with Sarah, he's been keen to be sexually upwardly mobile. But people tend to like Ken. Most of his fan letters are from women and are flattering – except for objections to sweaters without shirts. The only jewellery Stephen wears is one plain ring. 'This year, though, I wanted a bigger medallion for Ken and the costume people came up with this real horror – about the size of a coffee saucer with an anchor on it!'

Stephen is jolly and full of fun, but his eyes are serious, and it is not too much of a surprise to learn that he is quiet and even reclusive. He has recently bought himself a small 250-year-old house in a hamlet in the remote French countryside of Lot, and he takes off for it whenever he can. 'I love going there, just to be quiet and to think, and to do a bit of painting. I use watercolours, and I like to paint buildings. I get down there as often as *Howards' Way* allows, but I expect when the series comes to an end and I'm out of work I'll be spending quite a lot of time there!' Painting is a recent hobby, and he is teaching himself. One of the problems he may have to face is that *Howards' Way* has now been sold to France, so that he may be recognised there. 'Not that I mind, but I'm six foot three and bald, so I'm a bit hard to miss, and as one in four people in Britain watch *Howards' Way* I do tend to attract a bit of attention when I'm out!'

Shooting a scene for
Howards' Way

Another hobby is running, which he takes seriously enough to have competed in both the Paris and Munich marathons. 'But I've slacked off a bit recently, because it was becoming a bit of a drug. I found that I was having to run nine miles a morning before I could get started on my day.' He still does two three-mile runs a week, and plays squash, tennis and cricket, so it's not surprising that he manages to keep slim. He is a good sailor, too, having spent many holidays on the Broads as a child. Unfortunately, Ken has more to do with power boats than yachts. 'The power boats are quite fun, though; they're very fast. I don't drive the big ones myself – that takes a lot of skill and experience – but even the smaller ones are exhilarating, and you have to know what you're up to.' He prefers sailing and of all the cast he is probably the one with the most experience, having sailed the Channel and done a coastal navigation course. Long before his connection with *Howards' Way*, his ambition was to buy a yacht and sail slowly round the world, something he still wants to do.

Stephen also designed the new *Howards' Way* sweatshirt, which sold out three times over at the Boat Show, but he doesn't like dressing up himself, and spends most of his time in track suits. 'I seldom wear an ordinary suit, though I have got a floppy Betty Jackson one. I suppose I ought to buy one of those Henry Rose suits. I was up for a commercial the other day for something respectable and the casting director was horrified: "Where's your suit?" she said.' He likes the fact that Ken doesn't have to wear suits much either, but supposes that if business success takes him into offices and boardrooms he might have to put them on more often. 'After all, he's become a paper millionaire – whatever that is!'

We don't know much about Ken's taste in music, but Stephen likes jazz, especially Count Basie, Duke Ellington and Oscar Peterson. He reads James Baldwin, F. Scott Fitzgerald and Zola. You wouldn't think he'd be very interested in cars, so you might be surprised to know that he drives a Renault GTA V6 Turbo – the incredibly expensive sports car Renault have introduced to rival Porsche. 'It's a penile extension,' he says with a grin, 'but it's useful for nipping down to France, because it's quite quick.'

SARAH-JANE VARLEY

Sarah-Jane plays the kittenish Sloane, Sarah Foster. Since the suicide of her husband, Mark, Sarah has been sharing not only Ken Masters' bed (this affair comes to an end early in series four) but also the business, Leisurecruise plc, in which she has a two-thirds interest. The impression the character gives is of a hard but very sexy lady. Sarah-Jane doesn't give the impression of being hard, though one's guess is that her background and that of the character she plays are similar. She looks like a dancer though, and it comes as no surprise to discover that she went to Elmhurst Ballet School in Camberley, where she stayed until she was seventeen. Once again, she is someone who came to acting almost by chance, through being cast in *Mr Quilp*, the musical version of Dickens' *The Old Curiosity Shop*. 'It was an absolute flop, but I had fun doing it!' That was when she was still at Elmhurst; she went on with her training at the Guildhall School of Music and Drama at the Barbican. One of her earliest television leads was also in a Dickens dramatisation. She played Estella in *Great Expectations*, made, as is *Howards' Way*, at the BBC studios at Pebble Mill. There was film work, too – *And The Ship Sails On*, by director Federico Fellini. 'He was a brilliant man to work with, but it was all quite chaotic.'

Sarah Foster was originally written as an older woman, but when director Keith Washington saw Sarah-Jane he was so impressed that he arranged for her to meet Gerry. Fortunately her husband had not yet been cast, so the character was changed to suit her age. Sarah Foster wasn't introduced until series two, and Sarah-Jane was very nervous at her first meeting with the established members of the cast, 'but everyone was marvellous and went out of their way to make me feel welcome. I do remember when Stephen and I first had to do a scene where we kissed. The kiss came at the end of the scene and we didn't actually do it until we

Sarah-Jane as Estella in *Great Expectations*, with Gerry Sundquist as Pip

had to, but he couldn't have been more helpful or more professional.'

She hasn't found that people in real life have reacted adversely to her since Mark Foster's suicide, though at an all-female lunch party of her mother's friends she was looked at a little askance. 'But that's all, and all the letters I get are friendly ones.' Viewers have become much more sophisticated, and no longer confuse the actor with the character. 'But there is one man who writes me poems.'

Sarah-Jane lives in London, in Chelsea Wharf, where she and her boyfriend are doing up a house they've bought. 'It's been going on for two years now and sometimes we wonder if we're ever going to get it finished.' They are so busy with it that she doesn't get as much time as she'd like to pursue other interests. 'I love music, especially Mozart, and I'm just beginning to listen to opera. I have a friend who's a member of the English National Opera, and he sent us tickets for *La Traviata*. It's good that opera singers look like real people these days, instead of houses.' She still likes to go to dancing classes, and is also keen on keeping fit. She has no plans to do any more dancing professionally, but she likes to keep in touch with that world. Other hobbies include cooking, especially French and Italian, and one of her specialities is duck à l'orange with limes instead of oranges. 'But getting the house together is what takes up most of my time and I love doing it and choosing the fabrics and the wallpapers.'

Her clothes are comfortably chic, setting off her stunning figure: 'At home of course I wear jeans most of the time.' She enjoys shopping for Sarah's clothes, and says she would wear most of them herself if her lifestyle meant dressing like Sarah all the time. 'I haven't really taken advantage of the thirty per cent discount but I did buy a silk dress from the last series. I've never worn it since, because every time I put it on I feel as if I'm putting on the character.' She loves dressing up for the evening though, and she is an avid filmgoer.

Sarah-Jane has a West Highland terrier called Whisky, 'but he's on holiday with my parents in the country while we're in the throes of decorating. I wasn't really a country person until I had him, but he's introduced me to long country walks, and I like them — they're good for losing weight, too.' When she isn't walking, she drives a Peugeot 205, but

On the set of *Howards' Way*

she isn't too fussed by cars, 'although I had my very first brand new one last year, and that was a rather special thing'.

She doesn't think she and Sarah Foster have much in common, though she finds much in her to admire. 'Sarah's very clear-headed and good at business; I'm not at all like that.' She might have been attracted to Ken by qualities she admired, but she told him that his qualities were no better than Mark's, and that Mark had other qualities which made her love him. His suicide was a tragic over-reaction. 'I think that it is important to like the person you play at least a little bit. And I don't think Sarah's a bad person, do you?'

TONY ANHOLT

If anyone has been dubbed the villain of the piece, it's Charles Frere, played by Tony Anholt. Tony's father was an insurance broker who worked in Singapore, where Tony was born. At the outbreak of the Second World War Tony and his mother were evacuated but his father remained behind, and subsequently he became a prisoner of the Japanese. He died on the Burma Railway. Tony was three or four at the time, and they were staying with some Danish friends in South Africa, having arrived there via Australia. At the end of the war they returned to London, where Tony has lived ever since. His mother remarried when he was eight. Coincidentally, his stepfather had also been a prisoner of the Japanese. There is no theatrical background in his family, except for a remote cousin who was an actress in Holland in the thirties and forties.

Tony left school at eighteen, having acted in school plays throughout, culminating in playing Hamlet. That clinched things as far as his future was concerned, but he didn't know how to become an actor. Then an emotional involvement sent him off in a totally different direction for a while. Briefly, he worked in his father's old insurance firm, then went abroad for a couple of years. His first stop was Spain, where he taught English and later worked as a courier for a travel company. That lasted for almost a year, during which time he learnt the language. He then moved on to Paris, where he taught English again and stayed for another year.

On his return to England, he married and took a job in publishing, but the acting bug was too strong to resist. He had packed a lot of experience into his twenty-three years, and he applied to three drama schools. He was accepted by two, 'but I was pretty arrogant at the time and didn't like the idea of going back to school, so I turned them down and took private lessons. I got my first work by spinning a line about a fictitious year I'd spent working in the business in the States. That got me into weekly repertory theatre at Folkestone, and I did twenty-six plays in twenty-seven weeks. That was the best possible training I could have. We did an incredible variety of plays. It was exhausting and stimulating, and I was earning £15 a week.' After a period 'resting', Tony joined the Lancaster-based Century Theatre, a touring company. 'Five pantechnicon trucks which converted into an auditorium, with a stage, a foyer, and dressing-rooms'.

Tony has since played more parts than he can remember, but recently in a winter break from *Howards' Way* he played Salieri in Peter Shaffer's *Amadeus*. 'That was a great challenge. You're on stage all evening, and the character has to go from old to young and back again, without make-up. I really felt I'd grown as an actor.' The stage remains for him, as it does for most actors, the place for real acting. He isn't superstitious, but he observes the theatrical superstitions. 'I don't whistle in my dressing-room, and when I say "touch wood", I make sure I touch it.' He likes to establish a fixed routine in his dressing-room. If the routine's upset, so is he. 'I might, for example, like a cup of tea while I'm making-up, and if I don't get it, it throws me.'

He is a much warmer and more humorous man than his character, but finds it relatively easy to bridge the gap. One of the most difficult things is to flesh out the part, and from the start he was anxious that the character should have some light and shade. 'I don't mind playing a baddie, but very few people are absolutely bad, and anyway one-sided characters are dull. Of course, there must be something attractive about him or Gerald and Avril wouldn't stay loyal to him.' He's pleased that the character is opening out more, and that he has been involved in that development. 'Charles is a man for whom life is a game which has to be won. It's good that his father has been brought in as a kind of sparring partner of equal, or even greater, ruthlessness. It also explains where Charles gets his personality. On the other hand, I think he must get his gentler side, his love of the arts, from his mother.' As the story unfolds, though, it is not without its shocks. 'I was caught a bit left-footed when I learnt that I was Abby's father – and just how that relationship works out remains to be seen.'

One of the main problems in an open-ended drama is that when an actor takes on a character, he doesn't know where the character is going or how it will end. 'Things can change as the scripts are written, and sometimes one can get quite a shock – for good or ill. But it does mean that you can't take your development too far in any one direction, in case it runs counter to what the plot later demands.'

Tony takes a careful interest in the clothes Charles wears. 'I remember when I first had to get kitted out, I'd just got back from touring a play in the Persian Gulf. One day I had to go shopping with the then costume designer, a fabulous woman called Sue Peck, before going down to Southampton to film. She'd done some research and looked out a few possibilities in Bond Street; after all, Charles is a millionaire, and he's not going to buy his clothes just anywhere. We went into Lanvin and bought stuff off the peg which was purposely not traditionally English, but which we hoped suggested the wardrobe of a rich and cosmopolitan man. We got suits mainly, but also blazers and slacks.' Sue Peck needed to ring the changes among the five or six principal men she had to dress – to have them all in business suits would have made for very boring television. In particular, there had to be a contrast between Gerald and Charles, so Gerald dresses very correctly in an English way. Ivor Danvers, who plays him, wears only club or college ties (usually Old Etonian), to contrast with Charles's European air.

Tony as Charles Frere

It's great fun going shopping for Charles, 'but it ruins your own shopping. They're terribly helpful in the shops because we're buying so much, and the other day the wardrobe people took me into the executive suite in Harrods. You are given a private room, they bring you coffee and a rackful of clothes, and you can change into things comfortably and privately. That's really how the other half lives.'

Tony wears smart informal clothes. 'When I started out, I was quite fussy about what I wore; I suppose I was very image-conscious. Then I went through a phase of reacting against that and wore any old thing. Now the pendulum's swinging back a bit, and I find I do enjoy shopping for clothes which look and feel good and make *you* feel good wearing them.' Suits are a part of his wardrobe, but the theatrical world is so informal that they are rarely required. 'I've bought a few of Charles's cast-offs. He's got all the good formal gear, and it's great to get it a bit cheaper.'

How rich is Charles? The implication is that he is very rich indeed, and must certainly be a multi-millionaire. 'I know that when we first filmed at the château, the director, Tristan de Vere Cole, pointed out that if Charles owned such a place he'd have to be so colossally rich that he'd be priced out of the series. We put in a line to explain that the château was owned by "the consortium".' The reason we see Charles only on his boat or in his study is that a house hasn't been found for him. One was arranged, but the owners and the BBC couldn't agree a facilities fee and it was abandoned. However, plans are afoot to resettle the poor man and by the time you read this you may be seeing him in a million-pound pad overlooking the Hamble.

Apart from one magical experience of sailing round the Cape of Good Hope in an ocean-going yacht some years ago, Tony has not had much to do with boats. Nor has *Howards' Way* brought him any closer to them. 'Confined spaces bother me, and I find the space in a boat very cramped after a short time. I remember filming on location in Venice once. It's a wonderful city, but after a few days I began to feel uncomfortable. I soon realised that it was because there were no open spaces – no trees, no fields . . . but if I could have a boat like Frere has in the series, I'd adore it.' The cruiser in question, on whose after-deck Charles has held so many

Left The delectable Jan Howard models one of the elegant outfits from her Collection
Below Avril the cool executive looks ravishing in her cream silk shirt

Above Polly looks stunning in a blue and white summer suit

n's first partner and designer Claude
upont (Malcolm Jamieson),
rrounded by some of his sketches
drawn in real life by Alistair Blair

'And thereto I plight thee my troth' – Claude and Lynne on their wedding day

Left The bride with her proud father
Below All is forgiven on a wedding day. Even Ken Masters gets a look in!

Above left The bridesmaids' dresses were by Sue Peck, who also designed the wedding dress
Above right A kiss for the bride's grandmother from admirer Jack Rolfe

Anna Lee (Sarah Lam) Claude's successor at the fashion house after his tragic death and *(right)* one of her sketches – drawn in real life by student Natasha Braby
Below Avril and Charles show off an Anna Lee 'original'

ANNA-LEE

A photo session for Anna's designs in the grounds of 'Highfields', Sir Edward Frere's country seat
Below Jan Howard – the housewife who became head of a fashion house after the break-up
of her marriage

Top left Cindy Shelley (Abby Urquhart) gets a dab of extra make-up during a shooting session on location

Top right All part of the job. Maurice Colbourne signs his autograph for a young admirer

Above left Lunch on location. Sian Webber (Emma Newsome) collects her meat-and-two-veg from the catering truck

Above right When you're filming, you spend a lot of time waiting. Edward Highmore and Sian Webber do their share

important meetings, is hired by the BBC. It was built by the American firm of Hatteras and costs something luxurious £500 000 to buy in England, but their models go up to £750 000. Charles's boat even has three bathrooms.

Charles has had a different car in every series: in the first it was blue, in the second red, and back to blue in the third. The first two were Bentleys, the third a Rolls, and the red Bentley was a step up from blue because it was turbo-charged. That looks like careful structuring, but it came about by chance. The red Bentley was all that was available when the second series was scheduled, but Tony begged not to be given a bright red car for the third, so he got his Rolls, since there was one available in blue. In real life he drives a Ford Granada, which he's about to change for a Renault 25. 'I haven't a business head at all, so I'm unlikely ever to live the kind of life, and have the kind of things that Charles does and has; but if a Hatteras boat or a Rolls-Royce were to drop in my lap, I don't think I'd have any trouble adapting to them – the only problem would be where to put them!'

'I like classical music almost exclusively, mainly Mozart and Beethoven [as does Charles], but I am interested too in classical Spanish guitar music, above all that written by Narciso Yepes. Sadly, I don't play an instrument myself.' But Charles would probably not be deeply interested in the teachings of Hinduism, as Tony is. Like Charles, he is very fit. He played football at school, and rugby for a short time afterwards, but gave it up because he couldn't take the obligatory sixteen pints after every game. 'I used to be something of an athlete. When I was at school I was chosen by Surrey to run in the all-England championships, and my best performance was running the mile in four minutes and nineteen-point-something seconds when I was seventeen. I was told I should have gone on because I had Olympic potential, but for one reason and another I didn't. I sort of regret that still, especially when I watch people like Seb Coe zipping around the track. I belong to a health club, but I can't say that I go all that often. I'm certainly not a keep-fit fanatic.'

One thing Tony has noticed is that because of the character he plays people assume that in real life he's loaded. Fan mail comes from all sorts of people, of either sex, aged between twelve and sixty. Most simply want autographs, some tell him their troubles, others again want advice or help about getting into acting. People write and ask for locks of hair '... and there are a handful of rather more personal offers, where telephone numbers are supplied. What it's like to be a real Hollywood movie star I shudder to think!'

SUSAN GILMORE

One of the most important love stories in *Howards' Way* has been the affair between Charles and Avril. Fraught with difficulties though it has been, it has developed into a fuller and more successful relationship than any other, if you consider Tom and Jan, Sir Edward and Jan, Ken and Jan, Ken and Sarah, Charles and Lynne, Tom and Avril, Leo and Amanda. Only Gerald and Polly have preserved a precarious even keel, without sex, though poor old Polly does her best. It looks as if Charles and Avril may well end up being the best-matched couple of the lot, unless Leo and Abby get their act together.

Avril Rolfe, the tough business woman with the soft heart and the nervous manner, is played by Susan Gilmore. Susan is a Londoner by birth and has lived there all her life, but her parents both came from Scotland and that is where she feels most at home. 'I've never felt completely English.' She comes from a theatrical family. Her father, James Gilbert, is head of comedy programmes at Thames Television, her brother is a TV comedy producer in Glasgow, and her sister is just beginning her singing career with a tour of Japan and Australia. 'We're a bit of a family troupe, but we've rung the changes on the surname, which is actually Gilbert. I wanted to keep my own Christian name, and so we went through the *Penguin Book of Surnames* and narrowed it down to Gilchrist, Gilbride and Gilmore.'

She wouldn't mind living in Scotland, but London is the market-place for work so that's where she stays. She has been happy to work north of the border, and recently played a dotty Norwegian in a thriller called *Maelstrom*, screened just before work started on *Howards' Way*. Acting has always been part of her life – her mother was in the theatre until she started a family – and Susan grew up in an environment peopled with Scottish writers, actors and directors. She learnt the clarinet and the piano, but she didn't go to drama school, electing instead to go to university. She read English at Bristol and, later, English and Drama. 'At first I didn't have any intention of going into the theatre, but one thing led to another in a natural chain of events, and I felt less and less desire to resist the flow.'

Once she'd completed her Honours course, she went on to the Bristol Old Vic Theatre School. 'My father had said, "Right, you're on your own from now on," but I'd managed to get a grant, and I'd do waitressing and things in the vacations. I think I temped for every oil company in London. The thing is, if you're determined, you can do anything.' She is pleased that her father didn't pamper her, believing that you appreciate more the things you've really had to work for. 'That might sound a bit Thatcherite, but it isn't and I'm not, remotely, but it's sound Scottish common sense. I know a handful of people from university who live on their investments and do nothing with their lives, and make no progress as people. I think that must be so boring.'

Her professional career began with the English-speaking Theatre of Vienna. 'We did *An Inspector Calls*. We toured Austria for four months, and I came home with my Equity card and a suitcaseful of Austrian schillings.' Work followed at Worthing, and within a year she was working at the National Theatre, doing small parts and understudying, and building her experience – 'It was wonderful to work on *Amadeus*, for example.' But the National didn't seem to be leading anywhere, and she learnt through an actor friend of her father's that the BBC were looking for a new actress for *Angels*. She applied for the part, got it and stayed with it for forty episodes, playing Elizabeth Fitt ('Misfit, as we called her'). It was her first television experience, and she welcomed the opportunity to get used to the new medium gradually.

More theatre followed, and Susan seems blessed with good luck. At the last matinée of the last show she was in – a Restoration comedy at the Orange Tree Theatre in Richmond, Surrey – there were two TV directors: one offered her a part in a *Miss Marple*, the other one of the leading roles in *Maelstrom*. 'Mind you, it wasn't just luck. My agent tried to dissuade me from working at The Orange Tree: "You'll only get £100 a week and no one will come and see you." But I'd been around theatre people long enough to know that Richmond is home to dozens of TV directors who might not want to make the effort to go up to the West End, but who'll cheerfully go and see what's doing at their "local". That little run of *The Man of Mode* did very well for me.'

'I seem to have spent half my life in TV studios.' In a professional career of ten years, she has barely been out of work, but she'd like to do more comedy. All her major television roles, including Avril, have been rather severe personalities, and she isn't like that at all. 'I'm not business-minded like Avril. I can't even count or do my times tables. I think if I met Avril I'd probably like her, but would she like me? She's a bit of a high-flyer; I'm more of a muddler. What I like about her is that she's honest and tries to be straight with people, but I do wish she had a little more sense of humour.'

Off-stage, recently, Susan's time has been occupied by her new daughter, Emma Sheridan, now just over a year old. Emma's father, Dan Topolski, was coach to the Oxford University rowing team. The 'Sheridan' isn't after the playwright, but comes from an Irish branch of the family. Susan loves sailing, despite two recent close shaves, both of which occurred in the Aegean. On one occasion, when she was on holiday with her sister and two friends in Rhodes, they decided to sail over to the Turkish coast. A storm blew up, taking them unawares, and they couldn't control the boat. The storm raged all night, but eventually the wind blew them towards the coast and they were able to cast anchor in the shelter of some rocks. 'In the context of *Howards' Way* I find sailing very relaxing, and I'm sorry that Avril doesn't have so much to do with boats now she's left the Mermaid Yard. I liked the way the *Barracuda* was developed, and how we then had the real boat at the Boat Show, and how reality began to take over from fiction.'

Reality and fantasy, too, can meet in the overlap between actor and character. 'We have a word for it: "blurring". Certainly Jan and I will say it to each other, if for example one of us sees the other in private dressed in something bought from the character's wardrobe. And some of the actors drive the same car in real life as their character does in the series. The same goes for the odd occasion when we accidentally call one another by our character's name.' Susan used to drive a Golf GTI – the same car as Avril – loaned to her free for the purpose by Volkswagen, but it was stolen from outside her house not long ago and hasn't been recovered. 'It had everything in it because we had just loaded up to go out for the day. The police couldn't do anything – apparently those little sporty Golfs are a magnet for thieves.' A replacement Golf was also broken into, and had its radio stolen. Nowadays she drives the new VW Passat.

As Susan continues to play Avril, the effect of 'blurring' intensifies. 'I think I was far more objective, more socially realistic, in the first series than I am now about what she wore.' Avril has gone up-market since moving from the Mermaid to Relton's, and there are so many more executive women now that the fashion market has had to recognise that few of them want the female equivalent of the trusty pinstripe. The knock-on effect is that Susan enjoys wearing the kind of clothes Avril now wears. Principal designers are Nicole Fahri and Max Mara – 'I like a touch of eccentricity rather than just the straight down the line conventional look.' Last year, she bought some of Avril's suits, which she mixes and matches, but even with the discount they're more expensive than buying them in the sales at half-price. What doesn't get bought just stays on the rails in the costume stores, and something worn by a star one season may appear a couple of years later on the back of an extra.

Although she dresses less casually for rehearsals, her private style remains her own. 'What I wear on any particular day depends on how I feel when I get up in the morning. Yesterday I wore jeans and a sweatshirt, but I might just as easily find myself putting on a short skirt and high heels. Since my baby daughter arrived I've dressed more casually and comfortably at home, but I still love dressing up when we go out for the evening.' She likes to add one or two little touches to a conventional outfit. 'I used to be very offbeat. I was a seventies child, and I grew up in the gap between hippies and punks, so I was a kind of post-hippy.' Her favourite shop is Cornucopia, but one of her treasured outfits is a forties suit she picked up at an antiques fair in Battersea for £12. She also has a glamorous evening dress made for *Maelstrom*, 'but we didn't use it because it's so tight I can hardly move and I was supposed to go crashing through the woods in it after I'd gone mad.'

Ever since she worked as a programme-seller at Covent Garden when she was seventeen, Susan has loved opera – 'although it all began as a mistake because I'd taken the job to see ballet, which I already adored.

Only I didn't check what would be playing.' Her favourite is *La Traviata*. 'I had it playing during Emma's birth – I find it so strong, so sustaining.' Work on *Amadeus* developed her interest in Mozart, who is now one of her favourite composers. She also loves travelling and has recently come back from Bali and Hong Kong: 'I wish we could have gone on to Australia but I missed Emma and wanted to get home to her.'

Susan enjoys public response to her. 'Perhaps it's something to do with *Howards' Way*, but the way people react to me is very positive, and I like it when they smile and are helpful. It's great when you're shopping at Sainsbury's and the guy packs your stuff and takes it to the car for you because he wants to exchange a few words about *Howards' Way*.' Fan letters are vetted, but most are requests for autographs, 'though there's one man in Birmingham who's been writing to me since I was in *Angels*; he's even written me a ballad.' The most frequent remark from people she meets is, 'Oh, it's my mother's favourite programme.'

Because of her Scottish connections, she has always felt an affinity with Norway and Sweden. There is a dark, brooding quality in the Scandinavian nature which she finds dangerous, but which she understands. She would like to tackle Ibsen, and especially Nora in *A Doll's House*, which she played at drama school. 'But I have been very lucky so far, I haven't had to scrabble around for work, and I've had enough financial security to develop my own life. In the theatre that's a privileged position; some actors go through their whole careers without reaching it.' She is well aware of the image of the struggling actress, living alone at forty in a rented flat, with maybe just a cat for company and holding on to the dream of stardom. 'I see people of my age still doing tiny parts in provincial rep for a few weeks a year, and the rest of the time they're hanging around. Their lives are going down the plughole, despite the fact that they are talented in other areas. I think women especially have a capacity to dedicate themselves to very foolish causes sometimes. I gave myself five years, but I promised myself that if I hadn't got anywhere by then I'd chuck it and try another direction. You need talent, but my God you also need luck.'

GLYN OWEN

Avril's father, boozy and cantankerous Jack Rolfe, was one of the first characters to be cast, because Gerry knew exactly whom he wanted. Glyn Owen had worked with him before, when he played Edward Hammond in *The Brothers,* but he has also had a distinguished career in television drama which stretches back to the fifties, when he first established himself as Dr Paddy O'Mara in a little short-run 1957 serial on ITV called *Calling Nurse Roberts* which, under its new title of *Emergency Ward 10,* ran for ten years.

Glyn was born in Bolton, Lancashire. His father was Welsh, and perhaps it was from him that he inherited a wonderful singing voice. In the school choir, Glyn became interested in acting. When his voice broke, he went in for amateur dramatics, and from there went on to his first professional job as an assistant stage manager at Dundee Repertory Theatre. After a short spell in Scotland, he went to London, where he was a founding member of the famous English Stage Company at the Royal Court Theatre. He stayed there from 1956 until 1960, and was in at the birth of the new drama of the 'angry young men', playing in Gwyn Owen's *The Keep,* and John Osborne's *Plays for England.* It was with another John Osborne play, *Luther,* that he went to New York in 1963. The play was a smash hit and ran on Broadway for six months. He also re-created for television the role of Conn in *The Keep.* A Londoner by adoption – 'I've lived here for forty years' – he returned to New York to play in another smash-hit transfer, *London Assurance;* but although he likes the bustle of New York, he doesn't think he'd like to live there: 'I'd get homesick. You see, I may look tough, but basically I'm a pussy-cat!'

Although he still loves the theatre, and returns to it whenever he can, it is as a television actor that he is best known. *Emergency Ward 10* was quickly followed by *The Ratcatchers.* His association with *Howards' Way* producer Gerry Glaister alone goes back thirty years, to the early days of

Dr Finlay's Casebook and *The Revenue Men*. In the live theatre, his favourite roles have been the headmaster in Colin Welland's *Roll On Four O'Clock*, and Claudius in *Hamlet*, opposite Tom Courtenay. Every year in the *Howards' Way* break, he returns to the theatre to do pantomime. 'There's nothing like the reaction a live audience gives you, and I wouldn't be without it. I can never get used to the ovation they give me when I walk on stage nowadays. But to get to the kind of audience that *Howards' Way* reaches in terms of numbers, you'd have to play every night in a theatre for several lifetimes.'

He is pleased that the public find Jack such a sympathetic character. 'Although I'm nothing like him. I'm not nearly as tough and abrasive, and I'm less stubborn too. I'd never have dug my heels in over wooden boats as Jack has. On the other hand, I can understand his feelings for them, and for the work that's gone into them, the sheer skill.' He tries to counterbalance Jack's toughness with a blend of charm and humour, which is probably why, however irritating they may find him, people always end up forgiving Jack Rolfe.

Glyn has not developed an interest in sailing as a result of the serial, but it is not the first time he has worked with boats. 'I was in a drama series based on the lives of lifeboatmen a few years ago, and that was when I learnt that a boat can come to have an almost human personality.' Although he has learned to handle boats, Glyn almost came to grief towards the end of the film sequences for series three. 'The story ran that Jack had been having lunch with his old flame, Vanessa, and lost track of time, making him late for the start of the Wolf Rock Race. Vanessa managed to persuade the power boat driver, Richard Spencer, to take Jack out to join the *Barracuda*. We had to film a scene where Jack has to cross from the power boat to the yacht.

'It was Cowes Week, and the Solent was like Piccadilly Circus. Eddie Highmore was on the *Barracuda*, and he was beckoning. He meant us to come closer, as the yacht was already under sail and we were both moving along at quite a lick, but I thought he meant I should jump across – so I did, and I damn nearly fell in! Luckily he grabbed me and I managed to cling on, but *Barracuda* was doing maybe twelve knots and you can't just put on the brakes with a yacht. I had about twenty quid in my back pocket and I kept holding on because I didn't like the thought of the money getting wet – but if things had turned out badly, I could have been killed.'

There is one superstition which he observes religiously: he will not open an umbrella indoors. 'There is a very sad reason for that. As a young man, I went home to visit my parents one Saturday, and did an impersonation of *Singin' In The Rain* for them, the full Gene Kelly bit with the umbrella. Three days later, my mother died.'

Work leaves him little time for hobbies, but when he relaxes he likes to listen to music. 'I like everything, from pop to the classics,' and he singles out as favourites songs by Cole Porter, Gershwin, Berlin, and Rodgers and Hart. 'And I could listen to Frank Sinatra forever.' Under the bluff exterior, you sense a shy man whose warmth makes the character of Jack Rolfe endearing. Vanessa, or maybe even Kate, may well come round to making an honest man of him one day.

NIGEL DAVENPORT

The other elder statesman of the serial is a very different type. Sir Edward Frere, the cold, calculating capitalist whose charm has recently unsettled Jan, is played by Nigel Davenport. Nigel and Gerry Glaister are not strangers to each other; they have known each other since the beginnings of their careers when Gerry was the artistic director of the Chesterfield Theatre and Nigel was its young leading man.

Sir Edward probably returned from semi-retirement in the West Indies when he got wind of how well his son was doing. Perhaps he felt a bit envious, or perhaps he just wanted to re-establish contact. Relations between father and son had never been good, and Sir Edward had always been a remote figure to Charles. Nevertheless, blood is thicker than water and Sir Edward might have entertained a wish to groom Charles to take over his empire in the fullness of time. When Charles wouldn't play ball, his father decided to teach him a lesson. This is speculation, of course. Much of the drama between the characters goes on off-stage. 'But one treads a fine line,' says Nigel. 'When I'm asked if I research a fictional character, I quite often reply, "Not a lot", because the character should be inherent in the script I'm given, and bits of background knowledge might get in the way.' But when he played George III in *The Prince Regent*, for example, Nigel delved thoroughly into his past.

'Sir Edward is based on my knowledge and observation of real-life tycoons, a few of whom I have met. One of the things I've found about them, for example, is that they are not generally very cheerful people. They are always thinking about the projects they're involved in, and if they are cheerful they exude a kind of false *bonhomie*. They also tend to dress soberly and conventionally; perhaps they like to appear industrious and responsible. They may go for the trappings of rich living, like Rolls-Royces, but they are rarely flash or even seem to enjoy their money. What

I think they do enjoy is the fight, the competition. I am sure that is what motivates Sir Edward. On the other hand I did meet one charming tycoon, now dead, who ran the scent company Goya. He used to describe how he started off making the scent in his bath. He sold the company twice; the first time, the purchasers made such a hash of the business that he bought it back at a considerably lower price than they'd paid him and built it up again.'

Nigel could pass for a humorous tycoon. He is a tall and imposing man, whose taste in clothes tends to be shirt and tie, quiet sports jacket and slacks. He was born in 1928, and is delighted that as an indirect sixtieth birthday present he has been included in *Who's Who.* 'I've mentioned that I'm twice divorced and now live alone, so that's in the public domain, but I have tried to keep my entry decently short.' He was the son of a bursar of Sidney Sussex College, Cambridge, and grew up in Cambridge, but went to Trinity College, Oxford, where he took part in university drama and appeared in plays with, among other people, Irving Wardle, drama critic of *The Times.* Before that he went to school at Cheltenham, where his younger son, now fifteen is studying. 'Actually just fifteen, and I'm in trouble because I forgot to send him a birthday card. Still, he knows what he's getting for his birthday: a skiing holiday. A friend of his has invited him, so his mother and I have got to divvy up!

'I started at Oxford reading PPE [Philosophy, Politics and Economics]. I was okay on the two Ps, but when it came to the E I wasn't too hot. My moral tutor called me in one day and said, "Why are you reading PPE when you're obviously going to be an actor?" I didn't know it myself at the time, but I took his advice and switched to English.' While at Oxford he met his first wife, Helena, by whom he had two children. The son of that marriage is now a journalist on the *Daily Telegraph*; the daughter an actress. He went straight into the theatre after graduation and, like Glyn Owen, was a founder member of the English Stage Company, though his first professional engagement was as an understudy/ASM on Noel Coward's production of his own play, *Relative Values.* 'I spent ten years working solidly and consistently in the theatre, but in the early sixties I really began to feel the need for a change, and in 1961 I was lucky enough

One of the historical characters Nigel has portrayed – Conan Doyle. Pictured with him is his real-life ex-wife, Maria Aitken

to get my first television part. Wendy Craig and I played schoolteachers in a romantic play called *I Don't Like You*.'

Four years of television work followed, and the logical extension was to work in films. Nigel's chance came in the 1964 film of *A High Wind in Jamaica*, in which he played the father of a group of children captured by pirates; but the part which placed him firmly on the map came two years later, the Duke of Norfolk in Fred Zinnemann's *A Man For All Seasons*. Its success launched him on a career spanning another thirty-five films.

When he has time, he listens to Verdi and Puccini. He is fond of the pop music of the sixties, 'though I can't stand the modern stuff that passes for pop'. He also enjoys gardening at his cottage in the Cotswolds. 'My ambition is to establish a herbaceous border, but as things stand you'd have to describe it as work in progress. Never mind, I'll get there yet.' Since his marriage to actress Maria Aitken came to an end, he has lived in a little flat tucked away behind Knightsbridge in London, which he has had for twenty-five years: 'I hate moving.'

He is a keen horse-rider. 'I've ridden all my life, though less so now, because falling off's so much less comfortable when one grows older.' He also enjoys horse-racing and, by extension, Dick Francis's thrillers. 'I used to enjoy Kingsley Amis's novels, too. I adored *Getting On* and wanted to make a film of it, but I couldn't get to grips with *The Old Devils* at all.' He doesn't really have time for hobbies because when he's not acting he's running British Actors' Equity, the actors' trade union. He has been directly involved with Equity for about twelve years and president since 1985. 'I must say that one of the most awe-inspiring moments of my life was when I had to make a speech about the film industry at last year's Trade Union Congress. Preparing the speech wasn't too much of a problem, but standing up and addressing two and a half thousand hard-nosed trade-unionists was a pretty frightening thing, even after thirty-eight years' experience of audiences!'

IVOR DANVERS

'Poor old Gerald doesn't get near the boats much. The most he can hope for is the occasional business meeting on Charles's cruiser!' Ivor Danvers, who plays him, has been luckier. He was on holiday in Australia at the time of the bicentennial celebrations, and the crew of one of the tall ships that had sailed to Sydney from Southampton hailed him as a long-lost friend and welcomed him aboard – 'It turned out that they were all fans of *Howards' Way*.'

Ivor Danvers is the son of impresario Charlie Danvers, and his mother was a singer and dancer before she married. He is the youngest of five children, but despite their theatrical background Ivor is the only one to have gone on the stage. Both his children have followed in the family tradition however. Lindsey, his daughter, is a pop singer and cabaret artist, and his son, Tom, also known as Turk Thunderthrust, is the resident DJ at the Limelight Club. 'The only advice I ever gave to my kids was, "Don't worry about having to find a job that'll earn you a living; find out instead what you really want to do, and then do it to the best of your ability. You'll find you'll make a living out of it." What you need is a purpose in life, not just a pay cheque.'

Because his parents were moving around a good deal and he was growing up in wartime England, Ivor attended fifteen or sixteen different schools. 'I think my mother felt the Germans would find it more difficult to hit a moving target.' However, he is basically a Londoner, and has lived in Putney for the past twenty years, where he and his wife own and manage Henrietta's Restaurant.

'I am nothing like Gerald, though there are points of contact with the Urquharts I can find in my own experience. My father was much older than my mother and he was often away, so I can understand Abby's sense of isolation; and, because I have a daughter of my own, I can put something of that into Gerald's relationship with Abby. At the beginning, Gerald was rather a sketched-in character and I couldn't see how to play it. When I asked the director who'd cast me he said, "Play him enigmatically, for the moment!" They certainly hadn't conceived the character as a homosexual to begin with and it was quite a handful to cope with that and the fact that I wasn't Abby's real father after all.'

Gerald's scenes are mainly with Charles and Polly, and it was important to get the chemistry right there. One of the problems he and actress Patricia Shakesby, who plays Polly, had to sort out was why their characters had stayed together for so long. They'd been together for twenty years, and so presumably they'd found a way of living together. A precise profession had to be decided upon for Gerald too, as well as an income bracket. Without such hooks, it is difficult for the actor to construct the character. All these things had to be hammered out as Gerald became part of the central *Howards' Way* company. 'There came a time when the scripts started to be written as I had been playing the character; and I felt that things were on the right lines at last.'

Ivor on the boutique
set with Patricia

Ivor is a keen golfer, and through the game often meets men in the same business as Gerald – finance and the law – so that he has plenty of opportunity to observe dress and mannerisms. 'Gerald always wears a tie, and that is something I have noticed in real life. My father-in-law, who is a retired chartered accountant, always wears one and, like Gerald, it is rarely other than a club or college stripe.' Ivor dresses casually and comfortably. 'I guess you could call me a pullover-and-slacks man!' He belongs to Richmond Golf Club, and was recently president of the Stage Golfing Society. 'I've never been a sporty type, but a mate of mine who's a writer got me interested about fifteen years ago and I've been playing ever since. It's a nice thing for an actor to do, because it gets you out into the fresh air when you're resting, instead of mooching around waiting for the phone to ring! Even when you're working it's good therapy to get out and concentrate on hitting a little white ball into a series of holes.' He also plays bridge (he was a county master) and, among the comfortable scatter of books and paintings in their flat above the restaurant, there is a much-used computer chessboard. 'I think I have the kind of mind that latches on to strategic games. I certainly don't have much academic education. I went to the Italia Conti Theatre School and as my father died when I was seventeen I had to go out and earn a living. We weren't by any means well off.'

His first job was as a thirteen-year-old, in the chorus of a production of *La Bohème* at the Cambridge Theatre, and he has been acting more or less continuously ever since. His voice served him well until it broke, and then there was a brief departure from the stage when he joined the Merchant Navy. 'I signed on as a steward on a passenger ship, but I didn't know about giving backhanders to the chefs to ensure good service, and I wasn't very good at serving table anyway. I kept dropping forks, so I lasted precisely one day. Then they put me on silver-polishing duties. The boat was bound for Australia, so it was five weeks before I could get off.' In fact the job lasted six months. 'But I remember some time after that going to see a play, and afterwards I noticed a couple of the actors leaving the theatre. They were talking, and they looked so excited and alive. I knew then – though I sat up all night thinking about it – that an actor was exactly what I wanted to be. Before that, I'd sort of drifted along. Now I was convinced.'

He has done a lot of musical work, and one of his favourite roles is Professor Higgins in *My Fair Lady*. 'The songs are wonderful, but technically they are devils.' He played the title role in *Alfie* at the Richmond Theatre, and directed several productions there. He also played Reg in *The Norman Conquests* in the West End, a job he remembers with pleasure. 'And a few years ago I rediscovered that I could sing a bit, doing a musical called *Noel and Gertie*, about Noel Coward and Gertrude Lawrence. I've got a rather strapping light baritone voice, quite loud.' In the restaurant, he and his wife play recordings of thirties dance bands (the restaurant is inspired by thirties motifs), and his taste in music tends to be from that time. 'I could tell you practically the whole cast of any film from the thirties and forties too.' He sings a lot, to himself, whether he is happy or sad. 'I love Fred Astaire, but I have to say that my all-time favourite singer is

Frank Sinatra.' He pauses to dust a large and clearly adored cat, Moggie, off his knee.

For all the troubles that beset him, or probably because of them, Gerald receives many warm and sympathetic letters, and there was no antagonistic response to the revelation that he was gay. 'I was worried about the possibility at the time, especially as the script mentioned that his friend died of AIDS,' says Ivor. 'It's such a delicate subject, and not one to treat lightly.' When people do write in to complain, he has noticed, it is usually to point out mistakes in continuity. 'Some people must watch like hawks! I remember in one scene when Gerald is supposed to have come back from Zurich, I introduced a bit of stage business where I brought Charles a bottle of duty-free booze. I put it on the desk, but there was nothing in the script to cover it, so Tony Anholt didn't refer to it. I got a letter saying, "I do think Charles treats you badly. You brought him a bottle of Scotch from Zurich, and he never even thanked you for it!"'

PATRICIA SHAKESBY

Patricia Shakesby, who plays Polly, was born in the East Riding of Yorkshire, but came to London when she was sixteen to join her sister, then a dancer at the Ballet Rambert. 'I came more or less *en route* to university. I had a place at Oxford, but ended up staying in London and went into the theatre instead. I'd already decided that I wanted to be an actress, but you didn't tell people in Yorkshire things like that; they'd look at you as if you'd told them you'd decided to go to the moon!' She had made her decision by the time she was six. 'I saw a production of *As You Like It* at the New Theatre in Hull, and that was it. I discovered Shakespeare and the theatre all in one.'

She still lives in London, and has recently moved to a little Georgian alms-house in Mortlake. 'Nothing like Polly's place, though I have done my best to improve her taste in interior décor since we first met.' It was at Patricia's instigation that the Urquharts' house was redecorated, and decent pictures replaced the prints which had been on the drawing-room walls in the first series. After all, she argues, the Urquharts are well-heeled and cultured people, and this should be reflected in their taste.

Polly is too bright to be just a decorative housewife, and a lot of her problems come from boredom. This is not an uncommon situation for women, as has been proved by the number of letters whose writers identify with Polly, and who write to her for advice. 'It is quite upsetting to have to explain to some of those poor women that Polly's situation isn't mine. In fact, my situation is the reverse of hers: I am unmarried and I work.' In one sense, Polly is a victim of her own affluence, because even if she takes a job she doesn't need to earn a living.

Patricia went into repertory theatre at Great Yarmouth when she was sixteen. 'I'd been in *Where The Rainbow Ends* which Noel Coward directed, and when I asked him if I should try to get into a drama school he simply said, "Don't waste your time, dear," so I didn't.' Television parts began with *Emergency Ward 10*, and *Coronation Street*, though she continued to work in the theatre. She has rarely been out of work in a career which spans nearly thirty years. 'Work isn't everything to me though, and although I live alone I am actually quite a family-oriented person. I lost both my parents last year, which was a bad blow, but I am close to my sister's family and as she lives in Kuala Lumpur I brought up my three nieces when they were at school here. They are twenty-six, twenty-four and twenty-two now, and have children of their own, so my sister has come here to take a degree at the Open University. She's reading Fine Arts and Sociology. Which means that my adored great-niece, Lauren, who's three, and I are the only members of the family who haven't yet gone for a degree!' Patricia was married briefly when she was very young, but has not felt tempted to try again. She has a long-term companion, a French diplomat, whom she frequently visits in Paris, 'but I don't suppose we'll get any closer. I couldn't live there and his work means he can't live here.'

As Polly

Although she has contributed a lot to Polly's taste in clothes and décor, her own, she says, is quieter. 'I have always been interested in clothes and I love the fashion side of the work, but Polly's lifestyle isn't the same as mine. I usually work in a skirt and jumper. I don't think I could stand being dressed up to the nines all the time like she is.' Most of Polly's clothes cost in the region of £300–£500. 'I have bought one or two things which originally belonged to Polly, but most of her stuff is out of my range!'

Nearly all her hobbies revolve round the arts. 'I love going to the theatre, especially Shakespeare – I'm actually a Shakespeare freak. I like opera – Verdi, Mozart, and Richard Strauss, and German music. I've worked a good deal in Vienna and often go there to stay with friends, so I hear as much music as possible when I am there. I think Vienna is still the music capital of the world.' Patricia has acted there in the English-speaking Theatre, but has also played in German. Her French and German are 'quite good', she explains modestly. She buys modern paintings when she can. 'I got an Elizabeth Counsell last year for £400, which I should think I could sell now for at least £4000.' She also enjoys reading about art and the theory of art, and does some drawing herself. 'I love reading. I'll read bus tickets if there's nothing else. I think I like to read anything except science fiction and cowboys and Indians.' Favourite authors include Graham Greene, and the Victorians. 'I like Dickens and George Eliot, and I can tell you that once when I was ill for some time I read the entire works of Anthony Trollope, in chronological order. It was about three hundred volumes, but I adore him so much that I'd do it again. And I guess I know every word of Jane Austen by heart.'

Despite Polly's image, which hasn't always been endearing, a high percentage of her fan mail is from children, who seem either to feel sorry for her or simply like her clothes. 'I've had very few unpleasant letters for Polly. Oddly enough, it's the English Rose characters who usually get the hate mail – it's called the Deanna Durbin syndrome. When they think you look as pure as the driven snow, certain people want to write in to shock you. When you look as if you can take care of yourself, they don't. Deanna Durbin got more hate mail than any other star ever. I've had nasty mail in the past when I've played that kind of part.'

CINDY SHELLEY

In real life, Patricia Shakesby and Cindy Shelley, who plays her daughter Abby, get on very well. Patricia was once required to slap Cindy in a scene where Polly and Abby were having a row, and she had to steel herself to do it. 'Patricia hates violence, and she couldn't bear to hit someone she likes. By the end of the scene she was in tears,' says Cindy.

Cindy is about as unlike Abby as Patricia is unlike Polly, but as the looks and the voice and some of the mannerisms are the same, some 'blurring' occurs in your mind as you talk to her. She was born in Arkley, Hertfordshire, the daughter of a property developer, and now lives in a garden flat in Hampstead, London, with her actor husband, Philip Shelley, and two cats, called Mogway and Burr. Mogway is named after one of the gremlins in the film *Gremlins*, and Burr is named after Raymond Burr, 'because he looks like him'.

She decided to be an actress when she was fourteen, after playing Joan of Arc in Jean Anouilh's *The Lark* at school. She later took her 'A' levels at Millfield, and then went on to drama school, where she met her husband. They began work together touring for a year with Polka Children's Theatre, 'which was a long haul, but a lot of fun too'. A bleak patch followed, but television parts trickled in with appearances in *The Young Ones* and *Three of a Kind*, and then she was offered the lead in a Shirley Gee play called *Long Live The Babe*. She played the part of Alice Courtenay in *Tenko* for a year after that and then, after a brief return to the live theatre to do a play for Foco Novo, she joined *Howards' Way*. 'I took some time off after series two to get back to theatre because by then I'd done three years of solid television, and I felt I needed some more theatre experience, but I tried my luck at a terrible time. I had a few offers, but there was nothing I really wanted to do and work for the sake of work wasn't the object of the exercise.'

Abby is the character whose development has been most obvious, and after a period in the United States she is a transformed person. Gone are the offbeat clothes and the unflattering haircut and, although she is still recognisably Abby and still not quite steady on her feet, she is more determined to stand on them now and has a career and ambition. 'I think having the baby has given her more confidence, and that through William she has learned how to give love. So she is much better at coping with the difficult human relationships which surround her.'

'It's good to see Abby tougher and happier, and it's fun to see her in smarter clothes.' Cindy is now letting the costume department get on with dressing Abby without her advice – 'I think I gave her too much of my own look in series two, which is to say twenties and arty. I shop for myself at Hyper Hyper and antique stalls, and I want to get away from that for Abby. I like wearing the clothes she's wearing now, as costume. Who knows? I might even follow her lead.' Abby is now dressing at Ralph Lauren and Viyella. 'I love the shopping – they treat you like a god!'

Left Cindy as Alice Courtenay in the successful BBC series *Tenko*. She is seen here with Claire Oberman as Kate Norris and Emily Bolton as Christina Campbell. *Below* Cindy being made-up. *Below right* Abby's new career – photographer?

'I'm glad, too, that Abby is getting away from the old image. The press cottoned on to it and decided that Abby was sad and weak, just because she was depressed and up against it. That got me down. And it's good that she's living at Highfield as Sir Edward's guest, because he's a new character for her to spark off, and they spark off each other pretty well.'

Cindy likes the Rolling Stones and Lone Justice, but suspects that Abby would prefer Mozart. 'And at the moment I'm devouring Ruth Rendell's thrillers, which I somehow don't think would be Abby's cup of tea either.' Although she enjoys playing the part, she's not sure that Abby and she would get on if they met. 'I'm much more easy-going than she is. She'd always stick to her principles. I'd always take the line of least resistance.'

One thing neither of them has done much is sailing, though they are both beginning in series four, when Leo takes Abby out in the new boat *Spring*. 'I'm looking forward to it. So far, I've only been in the water, not on it.' She really did jump into the sea for the suicide attempt. 'I wasn't wearing a wetsuit either, because I wanted to shiver when I came out. We did the take, and then they had to ask me to go again because some RAF jets had flown past during the first one.' For the shots of her in the sea, they put on wetsuits and went farther in. Two divers supported her arms while an underwater cameraman filmed her: 'No studio mock-ups for us.' Afterwards the director rewarded Cindy and Edward Highmore with two bottles of champagne 'for doing such sterling work'.

Summery as it may look on film, half the time it's freezing and the actors wear thermals under their summer dresses.

For the future Cindy would like to go back to the theatre and play some of the classical roles, especially Ophelia and Juliet, but also one or two of the darker Elizabethan heroines. For the time being, though, she is happy to carry on with the part of Abby, which she finds rewarding and interesting. 'And I've recently taken up jogging on Hampstead Heath, which is pretty near our home, and I've started to play the piano too – so I'm keeping pretty busy.'

CHAPTER FIVE

Under Sail

~~~

Putting thirteen fifty-minute episodes of television drama together is not an easy business, and it calls for careful planning and hard work from everyone concerned. No one can afford to be late for any 'call', and no one can afford to be off sick. Someone has said that the closer you are to the camera, the less likely you are to be either of those things. The tightness of the schedule is another reason for Gerry to see his role as that of 'benevolent dictator'. Overall consistency and style can be achieved only by one man making the key decisions and giving the key orders.

The serial is very much Gerry's baby because he created the characters and the framework. From the word go it was to be a glossy, up-market production, featuring brave men and beautiful women. 'Everything has been selected to look good,' he says. 'The cast are all very easy on the eye, and that is quite deliberate – as is the sunshine, the emphasis on the outdoor life. People watching *Howards' Way* as they do at the onset of autumn can escape back into summer for a while.'

Each series is mapped out as an overall story, schematically covering all the storylines. This is a loose framework developed by Gerry, the script editor and the script consultant, who also have responsibility for consistency and continuity, though changes can occur as details are worked out. From this the framework of each episode is determined, and it is then that the scriptwriters are brought in. These are usually experienced workers in a rather specialised field. They are carefully picked, for they have to care about what they're writing and believe in it. Gerry likes to give each writer two or three consecutive episodes, because they get a better grasp of continuity and room to develop their storylines. Precise details are left to the writer to work out, but he knows where his section of the story begins and ends, and what must happen in it. The writers are, however, given as much scope for invention as possible. They liaise with each other as they hand over, so that a constant check is kept on story continuity, characterisation and style. It is important, for example, that the verbal mannerisms of a character are maintained from writer to writer.

Howards' Way has developed its own distinctive house style, and new recruits to the writing team can pick it up from existing scripts and videotapes of the preceding series, which are stored in the producer's office in London. Duplicate copies are held in the BBC's comprehensive video library. These are also useful to new directors coming on to the series. Gerry explains: 'They bring an input of fresh ideas, and if directors and actors become too familiar they can make each other lazy.'

The production year for the cast is from February to October. Filming is done in the summer, to take advantage of the little good weather we get, and is sandwiched between blocks of studio sessions. Thus, for the earlier episodes the film content is done post-studio, and for the later episodes it is done pre-studio. As there is very little time between completing the episodes and their transmission, the last two episodes of each series contain a higher content of film – up to fifty or sixty per cent. This means that studio time is reduced and time taken for studio and rehearsal work is effectively halved. A fortnight is saved, which can be used for post-production (editing, dubbing and so on). Even so, the schedule is so tight that the last episodes are finished and ready for transmission only three weeks before they appear on screen. There is no room for faults, and efficiency is high. By early July the first five episodes are ready for editing, but the final episodes are still being made as the first are being broadcast.

The studio scenes are shot in two-day sessions (see table). Usually the sessions cover one episode each, but increasingly the system is changing to multi-episodic recording. This means that a number of scenes from different episodes, directed by the same director and which take place on

SERIES 4 AT A GLANCE

Episode	Director	Rehearsal period	Studio dates	Filming dates
1	Tristan de Vere Cole	12–23 Feb	24/25 Feb	2–11 May
2	Tristan de Vere Cole	27 Feb–8 Mar	9/10 Mar	
3	Alister Hallum	12–22 Mar	23/24 Mar	22 May–3 June
4	Alister Hallum	26 Mar–5 Apr	6/7 Apr	
5	Roger Jenkins	9–19 Apr	20/21 Apr	12–20 May
6	Roger Jenkins	4–14 June	15/16 June	
7	Alister Hallum	18–28 June	29/30 June	22 May–3 June
8	Roger Jenkins	2–12 July	13/14 July	16–19 Aug
9	Graeme Harper	27 Aug–6 Sept	7/8 Sept	25 July–15 Aug
10	Alister Hallum	10–20 Sept	21/22 Sept	21–26 Aug
11	Alister Hallum	24 Sept–4 Oct	5/6 Oct	
12/13	Graeme Harper	8–18 Oct	19–21 Oct	21–26 Aug and 9–11 Sept

the same set and use the same actors, are shot in a block, regardless of sequence. This makes production rollover more efficient, because it cuts down on actors' calls and means that sets do not have to be struck and set so often. The drawback is that scenes shot like this are often done well out of sequence, which places greater demands on the actors. Recently at Pebble Mill, Stephen Yardley and Sarah-Jane Varley, in the middle of doing scenes from episode two, had to add a couple of scenes from episode seven – the only scenes from that episode written so far. Difficulties of continuity are compounded too, for the make-up and costume staff. Practically every time an actor or actress leaves the studio, Polaroid photos are taken of him or her – back, front, and both profiles – as continuity reference shots. Continuity also has to register what an actor is wearing in a scene. A filmed scene and a studio scene which immediately follows it may be shot weeks apart, out of order, but you can't have the actor go through a door at the end of one scene dressed in red and come out at the beginning of the next wearing blue.

There is little backstage glamour at Pebble Mill. The building is a grim example of post-modernism, and the cast have cell-like dressing-rooms. There is no 'green room' for them to relax in, only a broad corridor outside the studio, with huge plate-glass windows on one side, which means that they freeze in winter and roast in summer. Even Gerry has to share a tiny, windowless cell with his production associate, dominated by a big TV screen showing what's happening on the studio floor.

Prior to each studio session, there is a ten-day rehearsal period in London, where the scenes are 'blocked' – the actors work out their moves with the director – and camera angles are discussed and decided. On the last Friday there is a technical run for camera crew and technicians to watch, after which there is a technical planning meeting. The producer gets a full 'Producer's Run' on the following Monday morning at 10.30 a.m., when all the studio scenes are run in story order. On the Tuesday there is a break, when people may revise their lines and perhaps travel up to Birmingham, then there are two studio days every other week on the Wednesday and the Thursday. There is a break from May to early June, and again in the late summer, when filming sessions take place.

The actors work hard. A typical studio day will start with a make-up call which may be at 9 a.m., and work continues until at least 10 p.m. Filming days are much longer, as so much has to be done in a short time and all the daylight hours have to be used. When they are away from home, actors are paid just £45 per night and the standard return rail fare. On location filming union agreements provide that they are fed by the company, but they have to pay for their own food in the studio. On location, the company is booked into the Polygon Hotel in Southampton (which provides a special BBC rate). There are rooms for make-up and wardrobe departments at the hotel, which means that actors can be dressed and made up before being driven to the chosen location in the unit coach.

Such is the need to maximise every second of time that one director may be working in studio while another is working on location; and film time is so expensive on location (at least £5000 a day) that one set of actors may be filming on a boat with one director while another director works with a different set of actors on land. You need a level head to work out the schedules. Not surprisingly, many people are involved. Apart from the producer's immediate staff, the directors, their staffs, designers and actors, there is a technical crew of thirty in studio. On location, apart from the cameramen, sound and lighting operators, and other technicians, there is also a specialised sailing cameraman for the yacht sequences shot from on board, and a location manager.

Where the cast stay on location – the Polygon Hotel in Southampton

Below 'Highfields' – Sir Edward Frere's country seat. *Right* Charles Frere's 'château' – actually in Aylesbury!

The location manager on *Howards' Way* is Jo O'Leary. Working alone, she is responsible for laying on locations, choosing a selection of them for directors to look at (it's called 'recce-ing'), negotiating facilities fees with owners of locations such as the real houses which are used for the exteriors of the Howards' and the Urquharts' homes (the BBC pays Tom Richardson £6000 a season for the Elephant Yard alone), and organising hotel accommodation for the cast and crew. A recent bonus for Jo was finding 'Highfields', Sir Edward's home. Set in the countryside away to the northwest of Southampton, it is no stranger to television (it was used in a recent dramatisation of *Mansfield Park*), but was discovered for *Howards' Way* by properties manager Don Cave. 'We needed a smallish stately home in its own park. I phoned a cousin who's a photographer in Bournemouth and he told me he knew just the place – he goes trout fishing there.' Don, whose properties budget for thirteen episodes is a scant £90 000, positively glows when he speaks of the beautiful furnishings already in the house. 'The money and the hassle we save by being able to film in such a place are unimaginable.'

One of the most expensive items in any film budget is locations abroad, and it looks as though *Howards' Way* has had several. In fact, there have been none. Various local locations have been made to double as parts of France and Italy, with the help of good weather and a little set-dressing. The Swiss bank interiors in series three were filmed inside Southampton town hall, and Charles Frere's Château Auban is Waddesdon Manor, near Aylesbury. 'We don't see it that often because the facilities fee is high,' grins Gerry. It was built by one of the Rothschilds as a kind of homage to Versailles, and looks completely French. Even Rhode Island, where Lynne arrived after her transatlantic sail, was re-created at Warsash on the Hamble. The director, Sarah Hellings, persuaded some US marines stationed nearby to appear, and she borrowed an American fireboat from a nearby base to add verisimilitude. A few establishing shots of New York were obligingly provided by the BBC's New York film crew, and the sequence was so effective that many people in the business were envious at the location perks *Howards' Way* seemed to enjoy.

Negotiations to film the shipboard romance between Claude and Lynne on the *QE2* while she was docked at Southampton fell through. The scenes were shot partly on the Isle of Wight ferry and partly on a local dredger, intercut with stock film which matched perfectly. The director, Tristan de Vere Cole, iced the cake by filming people disembarking from the *QE2* and cutting them in with Claude and Lynne's arrival home.

All the locations are close together. The farthest points apart are 'Highfields', Bursledon, and Lymington (where the marina shots are filmed and where *Barracuda* is moored). Schedules are arranged so that each is used for a number of consecutive days. Travelling time is wasted time. Most of the locations have disguised or unspecified names, and the production team tries to keep their whereabouts vague, partly to sustain belief in the fictional Tarrant and partly out of consideration for the owners, who do not want to have fans, however well-meaning, peering through their windows. Only 'The Jolly Sailor' is as it is in life, although the owners were offered a disguised identity. The result has been an enormous increase in business, and when the pub changed hands not long ago it fetched far more than it would have in its pre-television days.

eft Ken Masters (Stephen Yardley). *Above* Jan Howard (Jan Harvey)

Avril Rolfe (Susan Gilmore)

Charles Frere (Tony Anholt)

Kate Harvey (Dulcie Gray)

Above Jack Rolfe (Glyn Owen). *Above right* Lynne Howard (Tracey Childs)

Gerald and Polly Urquhart (Ivor Danvers and Patricia Shakesby)

Top Leo Howard (Edward Highmore). *Above left* Amanda Parker (Francesca Gonshaw)
Above right Abby Urquhart (Cindy Shelley)

Sir Edward Frere (Nigel Davenport)

Above Sarah Foster (Sarah-Jane Varley). *Above right* Michael Hanley (Michael Loney). *Top right* Emma Newsome (Sian Webber)

Below The exterior and interior of one of the mobile location trailers and the ladies who make sure the actors and crew don't starve

A good deal of transport has to be organised on location. The unit sets up a base in the car park of Bursledon Station. The restaurant coach is parked there, and there are make-up and costume trailers, a props van, a lighting equipment trailer, the unit coach, and a mobile toilet, as well as cars for the key production people.

The *Barracuda* is kept crewed and ready for use by Bob Fisher whenever she is required. Filming on board requires not only the actors but the director, his personal assistant, the cameraman, the sound man and the microphone-boom operator, as well as Bob Fisher and his men who do the real sailing. It is just as well that she is a fairly big boat. A safety boat shadows her, and a camera boat films her from the outside. On occasion, Gerry has also used helicopters, but at hire charges of about £500 an hour he cannot use them often. Gerry usually sets aside a few days when all the sailing sequences are shot. The actors not required for those sequences can be used for other scenes. This means two whole units and two directors working, but with careful handling money can be saved. Sailing sequences can be very costly if we are using boats other than our "in house'' yachts, *Barracuda* and *Spring*.' Getting all the sailing done in one go also means that there isn't constant worry about the tides, the wind and the weather – provided the right few days are chosen.

Costing is crucial. The danger of going over budget is constant, and for all its 12.5 million viewers *Howards' Way* is not a high-budget programme. It has a large cast of regulars, which bumps up the price, and creates a problem in getting foreign sales because of the residuals (repeat payments to the cast) involved.

The actors cannot afford to be ill. They can go off and do other jobs if they are not required, but *Howards' Way* has first call on them, and they must always be available in case there is unavoidable rescheduling. But accidents happen: Dulcie Gray broke her wrist but had to soldier on. On *The Fourth Arm*, another series Gerry produced, an actor broke his leg faking a parachute jump at Duxford. 'But I had him back on the set within a day. There was just no way we could stop or go on without him.' The only time which is marginally less important is fictitious time. Precise times and even sequences of days are deliberately kept vague. This helps in a series which has a nine-month break between each sequence of stories.

In 1988 the production year for the actors finishes on 22 October, but there is no let-up for the production team. By June or July a management decision will be made whether the serial is going to continue. If it does, series five will start production in February 1989 and Gerry's first job will be to make availability enquiries about the actors. If anyone doesn't want to continue, they have to be written out of the storyline. By September or October, the first scripts are being commissioned, the aim being to get the first eight scripts by Christmas, though they may be later due to rewrites. Old locations have to be reconfirmed or renegotiated, and new ones sought. If an owner sells one of the 'character' houses, and the new owners don't want to participate, that's another headache. If you think that keeping so many balls in the air is next to impossible, *Howards' Way* isn't Gerry's only project!

The *Howards' Way* rehearsal room is on the fifth floor of the dismal concrete block in North Acton which houses BBC TV's rehearsal facilities. It is a large, empty room rather like a school hall, with windows all along one side offering fantastic views over west London, making the town look like it does in early nineteenth-century prints.

All the studio sets are marked out in tape on the blue lino floor, different colours indicating different areas. Scruffy pieces of furniture are dotted about to stand in for the actual pieces: an old vinyl-covered sofa; a greasy brocade armchair with a castor missing. It's a long way from the luxe of *Howards' Way*. Vertical free-standing poles mark key turning points. like the limit of a wall. Scenes rehearsed here are only those which will be shot in studio at Pebble Mill. There are photos and drawings of the sets to help actors unfamiliar with them. Only the actors, the director and his immediate staff are present. The production manager takes notes. He has a small table covered in papers which he wheels to whichever part of the room they are using.

Because scenes are not necessarily shot in sequence there is some technical difficulty for the actors, especially as they do not have the full thirteen scripts to hand. It's like acting in a play where they do not know its dénouement. Such difficulties are ironed out at these rehearsals. For example, they run a scene where Charles arrives at Avril's house, interrupting a meeting she is having with Sarah. The problem is firstly a technical one: how should he make his entrance? Should he come through the kitchen or the hall to the drawing-room? Will the sofa be in the way of the camera? And how will they know he's arrived, because he has his own key? Should he call out? Should a door slam? The other problem is more serious. This is only the second meeting between Charles and Avril since the plane crash. The first meeting will be on film; they have not done it yet, and they have not seen the script. Yet it will have a bearing on how they respond to each other in this scene. What is the degree of their intimacy? The difficulties are compounded by the fact that the director is new to the show and not familiar with the characters. A long discussion begins.

The studio in Birmingham is a vast box, its ceiling festooned with lights: the 'grid'. Each light has a number. Typically, lighting director Bob

Chaplin will set seventy of them. Below, the sets are ranged around the edge of the box, facing inwards, where the cameras occupy a large central space. The sets look much older than they do on camera and slightly dingy. This is partly but not entirely because they are due for renovation; the camera enhances colour, so that colours as the eye perceives them must be toned down. The oldest set of all is the Howards' kitchen, which is bearing up well. Next to it, cheek by jowl, is the hall of their house, and beyond it the living-room and dining-room. Outside the windows are cycloramas with crudely-painted outdoor views. It's hard to believe it can be so convincing on screen. The Howards' fitted carpet only reaches half-way across the floor, covering just what the camera sees. Along another wall is Ken's Leisurecruise office. All the sets are half the size you might expect them to be, an indication of how well the camera can lie, as well as of how much we unconsciously add from our imagination.

There is only one television drama studio at Pebble Mill and it is in constant use. Overnight, two sets had been struck. Two sets are about the limit of what can be struck-and-set overnight without running into very expensive technicians' overtime.

Time in studio is of the essence, but the actors are aware of it and well rehearsed. Under an experienced director the scenes are got 'into the can' with surprising speed. The director will occasionally go down 'on to the floor' to talk to the actors, but most of the time he sits in his box in the gallery high above the studio, flanked by the vision mixer and his production assistant, who ceaselessly calls out the sequence of cameras and their shot numbers over the open intercom to the cameramen: '43 ... 3 next; 44 ... 2 next; 45 ... 3 next.' He or she faces a rank of television screens, but watches the one which relays the shot of the moment.

Typically a scene is rehearsed once or twice for the cameras and then shot. In the many little breaks there are fragments of conversation. 'Why is that camera smaller than the others? What's the difference?' Dulcie asks. 'Its size is the difference,' explains the director. 'It can get into the places the other cameras cannot reach.' There are frustrations. A good take is spoiled by the sound of drilling from a nearby building site. Someone is sent out to ask them to stop. Throughout, the director's concentration and eye for detail is astonishing, though he is tense and bawls out the lighting crew in the next box for their whispered conversation. He rejects a take: 'I was conscious of a loose hair on Dulcie's forehead – it's the kind of thing that distracts me.' Another time, there is a microphone-boom shadow on Edward's face.

Between takes, girls touch up the actors' make-up, putting little towels on their shoulders to protect their costumes. Leo's hair is sprayed into position; powder is dabbed on Ken's bald head: the heat from the lights has made it shiny. A props man pours drink back into bottles and washes the glasses. Champagne is weakly-made ginger ale, whisky is coloured water. Keeping an eye on the level of drink in a glass or the length of a cigarette between takes is the continuity girl's nightmare. Who hasn't seen films where they vary illogically from cut to cut? Attention to detail is vital, for once the scene is 'wrapped' it's almost impossible to undo any errors.

Production associate Tony Rowe has the unenviable job of policing the budget. 'It's about three million quid a series,' he explains, 'but many of the people who work on *Howards' Way* are salaried BBC staff, and their pay is met out of the departmental budget not the programme budget. Even so, the biggest slice of our cake goes on salaries to the freelancers, the most obvious of whom are the actors. We spend a certain amount on graphics too, which means the creation and printing of fictitious logos and letter-heads for example. Other big chunks go on location fees, design, and props.' Props, it should be added, cover everything from a thimble to a Rolls-Royce.

Rolls-Royce/Bentley lend cars free because of the exposure they get simply by being seen on the programme. They supply the model and make requested if that is at all possible. 'Gerry wants a soft-top Corniche for Ken. There's only one demonstration model in the UK, so I expect we'll get that.' Character cars, such as Kate's old Countryman, are hired from specialist agencies. That the car suits Kate is borne out by Gerry's observation that one in three elderly ladies in Southampton drive one! When it comes to brand-new cars, some of the actors have made arrangements with manufacturers for a car they drive privately and in the series, if the car fits the character. However, the manufacturer knows there can be no overt advertising of the car on screen, nor can any guarantee be given that it will be featured for a minimum amount of time. Such arrangements suit the artists and ease the hire element in the budget, but they can backfire. Stephen Yardley was lent a Saab for series three, but when Saab saw how the character was developing they decided Ken wasn't the kind of man they wanted associated with their product, and withdrew. Fortunately, Renault filled the gap with their top-of-the-range sports car, which Stephen now takes on his trips to southern France.

The difficulty of avoiding advertising is also shown in the problems the production team had with the competition power boat in series three. Its owner-driver, John Yeoman, did a sponsorship deal with Unipart on the strength of the boat's appearance in *Howards' Way*, on the understanding that their logo would appear on the boat on-screen. When it was explained that the BBC could not accept those terms, or any such editorial control, Unipart withdrew. They have since reconsidered and are still sponsoring

UNDER SAIL | 137

John Yeoman. Gerry's ruling now is that advertising of that type can be shown only in unavoidable situations, such as at the start of a race, where many boats carrying different advertisements are seen together. The sponsor's name must be blanked out when showing the boat on its own.

Tony Rowe is at pains to point out that he doesn't save money. 'I just don't spend it in certain areas so as to free it for use elsewhere. People think *Howards' Way* is a very pricey show, but it looks that way only because we are able to stretch our budget. We're pegged at about the same level as *Juliet Bravo*, though, to be fair, the cost of hiring a police car is as high as the cost of hiring a boat.'

The design department buys in a certain amount of top-quality clothes, but designers are also happy to lend their models for the exposure value. We have seen how money can be saved by 'cheating' on foreign locations. 'Whenever we can, we collect useful establishing shots,' says Tony. 'For example, when we go to Guernsey to film the power boat race we will also film some corners of the island which we can use later to suggest various European locations. There is a much more continental feeling about Guernsey than England, and we take advantage of that. The use of establishing shots like that – and we sometimes even use library film – is often all you need to say, "This is where we are."'

Designer Jim Hatchard and props manager Don Cave have been with the programme for three years. Its new demands on their expertise meant they needed to seek out contacts in the boating world, particularly in the Southampton area. They were sent off in the right direction by Bob Fisher, particularly where specialised items were concerned. Rarely did anyone refuse to help unless they got something out of it in return. 'If people know it's for television, they help. There's a great deal of good will,' says Jim.

Old contacts rallied round too, for despite the amount of care and attention put into every aspect of the programme things have sometimes got to be done on the trot. Jim designed the well-known Leisurecruise red-and-black leather sofa over the phone to the manufacturer, and it was ready in five days. 'The manufacturer knew what was needed for

Ken's character, and I explained that I wanted the office to be intimidating. You actually see Ken Masters types down there, selling power boats, and their offices often reflect the pizzazz of the boats they sell. But there's an element of pressure there too. I wanted to get that across on television, so I thought of an office which would look like the cockpit of a power boat.' Hence the long sofa, which echoes the seating around the sides of a luxury power cruiser. Ken's desk, with its red sides and its special grey inlaid panel, was specially adapted by the manufacturer from a production model. 'They were happy to do it, because it was for television. We've had plenty of enquiries about the desk, too.'

Jim and Don live in each other's pockets while the designs are being drawn up, so that props bought or hired match absolutely. There are two kinds of prop: action props are anything that moves, from a teacup to a helicopter; dressing props stay still. The fittings and the dressing props in Ken's office reflect exactly the red/grey/black tone of the whole, the brash elegance which is Ken's trademark.

They stress that everything you design for television has to be just a bit *more* perfect than it would be in real life, a couple of points over the limit, because viewers are very quick to pick up points they think are wrong. 'That's even more true when you're doing a period drama, but whatever it is, matters of design need to be pointed up. The new restaurant set, for example, is ten per cent posher than the poshest restaurant you'd find in the Southampton area.' They also have to consider that the main characters in *Howards' Way* are nearly all very rich indeed. The restaurant, their new baby, pleases them. It's an up-market Italian place, loosely based on one which exists. 'It's got a vaulted roof, because the idea is that it's in a crypt. Tristan's got a real taste for the Gothic and he loves that, though the whole place is actually in our own sort of bastard Romano-Graeco-Gothic-Byzantine style!'

Every item that dresses every set is accounted for down to the last teaspoon on a property form. In the main property companies in London supply them. 'Farley's, Newman's, Spiller's for paintings, Camden Furniture Hire, A and M for Victoriana and Edwardiana. You set up a rapport with your regular suppliers, and each company we use all the time has a man

Below On the new restaurant set. *Opposite page* The Howards' living room

who has a *Howards' Way* brief to look after our props and make sure they are available when we want them again, and to make sure they haven't been changed in any way – in the case of furniture, for example being re-covered.' It is crucial that there should be no change between episode thirteen of one series and episode one of the next, because in other countries *Howards' Way* may not be shown in batches of thirteen with nine months between them. 'We'd be lost if, say, the Howards' suite changed upholstery and then changed back again, so we're dependent on each company's *Howards' Way* "caretaker".'

Their design budget, to include man-hours, materials and props, is £250 000. Out of it they have to run at least fifteen stock sets and put in another twelve to fourteen single sets of the type which will be seen once only. The designers of a feature film would need £8 000 000 to do what they do. Some sets, like Gerald's study and Ken's flat, have been dropped because the story no longer needs them. So has Kate's cottage. It is a false economy to keep a set which only one character uses. Kate has been moved in with the Howards partly because that releases space and money for other uses. 'But there has to be variety, and you must get as much variety as possible out of the sets you've got. The storyline was stimulated by losing Kate's set and giving her a new centre of interest in the boutique, away from the Howards' house.'

Currently the main sets are:

Howards' kitchen
Howards' dining-room and living-room
Howards' hall
Leisurecruise office
Charles's study
Urquharts' hall
Urquharts' drawing-room
Pub interior
Mermaid office interior
Restaurant
Boutique
Avril's cottage
Jack's cottage

'We have to give a glossy appearance, and the way we cut our cloth is to make a set small and spend the savings on size on opulence and detail. Sometimes it's a balancing act. If you know you need a prop for at least five episodes, it's worth hiring it for the series because you get a forty-five per cent discount. Maybe it's cheaper to buy. There are a hell of a lot of props, and you just have to weigh each one in the balance.' Even so, a great deal of the *Howards' Way* stuff is hired rather than bought, simply because there isn't the space to store it or the money to maintain it within the BBC. Anyway, they don't know from year to year if there'll be another series, so they can't assess whether buying in furniture, for example, is going to be cost-effective. Occasionally disaster has struck: a prop returned to the hirer has got lost, or broken, so lines have been changed to fit or comment on the change: 'Oh, Jan's bought a new whatever.'

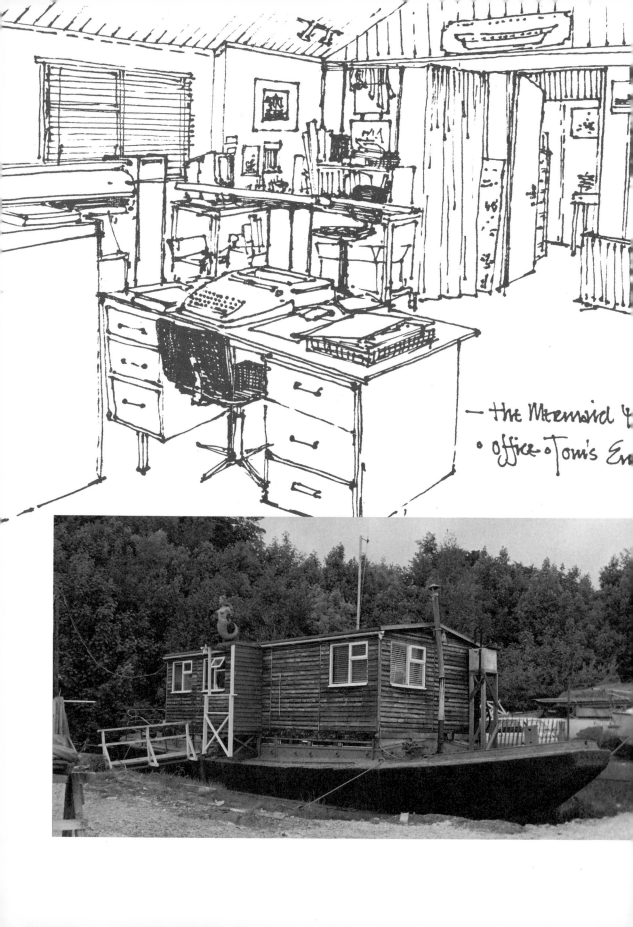

— the Mermaid [...]
• office • Tom's En[...]

There can be windfalls too. Don wasn't sure what kind of expensive vase Gerald should break in the scene where he loses his temper with Polly for extravagance. 'It had to look expensive, but I needed several because I didn't know how many takes they'd need to get it right. Luckily I got them from a firm in Stoke. It was a finished line and they let me have the last six for six quid each. They'd been selling for £35 in the shops.' Ivor, who by his own account cannot throw a ball, managed to do the business in just two takes.

Jim says the most important set they have is still the Mermaid office. 'It is a size-for-size replica of the real office down at the Elephant Yard in Bursledon. When I first joined the series, I thought no one could design a boat in the office as it was in our set, when it was the office of a boatbuilder rather than a designer. So when Tom came in and set out to design *Barracuda*, we needed to get his working environment right. We introduced a good-quality drawing-board, and then, later, the computer. The computer can be linked to the drawing-board.' At the Elephant Yard the office is built on the hull of an old barge, whose hold is the paint

store. The fictional Mermaid Yard mimics this, but when Tom gets a commission to design for the America's Cup (the most prestigious boat race in the world) the fictional hold will be converted into a high-tech computer room.

Detail is all-important to the design team. For the domestic sets, wallpapers and soft furnishings are bought from mainstream suppliers, especially the Designers' Guild and Mary Quant. They also use recherché suppliers who print papers and fabrics in desaturated colours: colours deliberately 'washed out' to give a faded effect because the camera enhances colour. 'A normal wallpaper is printed at the level of colour the eye receives, but if it's seen through a camera on a television screen it can look unnaturally bright. So we often buy papers and furnishings from manufacturers who do soft and pastel ranges.'

They receive thousands of letters a year enquiring where fabrics and set dressings come from, and they answer every one. Easily the most enquiries are about Polly Urquhart's curtains, which are a Sanderson material. Don is currently dealing with a request for the name of the supplier of the lace tablecloths used in the 1987 restaurant set, but they do have less straightforward queries. 'One woman wrote to us to say that the carriage clock on the chimney piece in the Urquharts' drawing-room was identical to one she'd had stolen from her. We made some enquiries, and it turned out to be her clock. The hire company had bought it innocently at auction, which it had obviously reached via various middlemen. So she got her clock back by watching *Howards' Way*.'

On another occasion, a man wrote in to ask about the marine painting outside the old boardroom set – a picture of a ship being launched. Jim had got it from BBC stock; it had been painted from a photograph some years earlier by a BBC staff designer for use in the series *Doomwatch*. The viewer who had written in was the son of the ship's original master and had watched her being launched. It was impossible to sell him the painting as it was BBC stock, but they sent him a photograph of it, and a photo of the artist. 'It's things like that which make the job for us, but really we do it because we love it.'

Apart from Gerry, the people with the longest uninterrupted con-

-JOLLY SAILOR-

JOLLY SAILOR

**— CHARLES FRERE'S —
· OFFICE ·**

nection with the show are the actors and the designers, and Jim and Don welcome any interest the artists show in 'their' sets. 'Patricia Shakesby really knows Polly's house. She insisted on having it redecorated, and she always knows the minute there's something wrong with the set dressing. There were some flowers in a vase once that were just too neatly arranged for Polly, so she muddled them up, much to the set-dresser's dismay! Patricia' s not too keen on her sets as they stand, but they have to be an approximation to the real house interior, in case filming from outside should pick up hints of the real interior through the window.'

They liaise closely with the location manager too. It can be that a location she chooses cannot be reproduced as a studio set because of difficulties of proportion. 'But it's great that we all work so well together as a team. People from outside too like to be involved with us.'

On the fashion side, they have had enormous help from luminaries like Yuki, Alistair Blair, Betty Jackson, Jeff Banks and Susannah Constantine, as well as Louis Férraud and Calvin Klein, who have all lent outfits and charged no more than the cost of cleaning. After all, if viewers see their clothes, like them, phone in to enquire about them, and can afford them? But the costume designers have always been realistic enough to include a

— NEW BOUTIQUE — PERIPLUS III.

number of smart outfits within the grasp of people who have less money to spend on clothes, and the *Howards' Way* women, though they may dress above average, don't wear the fantasy clothing created by Nolan Miller for the ladies of *Dynasty*. *Howards' Way* watchers may not be able to find the clothes Jan, Polly and Avril wear in every clothes shop, but they are accessible.

Music is a crucial element in *Howards' Way*, and Gerry was careful in his choice of composer. Simon May had worked with him before, and using him again has more than paid off. The *Howards' Way* theme has been in the Top Twenty twice – in its original series one version and again in the wistful series two arrangement, with lyrics sung by Marti Webb.

'My brief from day one was to write music that would not only provide a theme for the serial but also accompany certain characters,' says Simon. He had talks with Gerry to get a feeling for the programme and gathered as much material as he could about it and its background. 'I find it very important to get as deeply involved as possible to ensure that the music doesn't sound stuck on.' The main theme reflects the sea and links itself to the Howard family. It suggests an element of triumph in Tom's managing to overcome the misfortune of his redundancy. The acoustic guitar introduction then broadens the base to include the whole family. Following solid Wagnerian precepts, Simon has gone on to create themes for Frere, Abby and even the *Barracuda*. 'I wrote a sleazy saxophone motif for Ken and Dawn too, and even though Dawn's long gone the sax stuck with Ken for a while.' However, as the characters develop and change, so does their music: 'The thing is to hug the characters.'

To do this, Simon works from the scripts to do a rough recording covering all the episodes in a series. That is refined and honed as he sees the videos of each episode, to cover elements introduced in the production. After watching the videos and discussing them with the directors, he composes any extra music – 'I use a computer to help me, since it has to be done very quickly' – which is then dubbed on. The last lick of paint, the finishing touch, has been added.

CHAPTER SIX

Sail On

~~~

Howards' Way arrived at the same time as the kind of characters it portrays experienced a change for the better in real life. It is also popular beyond the dreams or expectations of those who created it. With an increase in leisure and more money being spent on it, the small-boats industry has increased in size. But how do these three things come together, and what is the *Howards' Way* effect on real life?

Chris Collman runs Quay Marine of Hamble, a business which features in the serial as Leisurecruise. When we see Ken's showroom, it's actually Chris's. Chris sells motor cruisers whose average price is £45 000. He is not short of customers. 'In reality,' he says, 'Mark Foster wouldn't have made a living selling top-of-the-range Class One power boats. The really professional ones, of the kind made by Cougar, cost around £200 000, and you don't get many buyers at that figure. There are only a couple of dozen in the world that really run competitively.'

Ken, in short, is on the right track. Power boating doesn't demand as much commitment as yachting because it requires less expertise. Chris's typical customer is the family man who feels he deserves a bit of relaxation and has done well enough to treat himself. The man who drives a Porsche or a big BMW may go for a cruiser, but it isn't only the rich who do. There are genuine enthusiasts. Chris knows one couple who work hard running a driving school. Every spare bit of cash and every free moment is spent on their power boat.

Chris got involved with *Howards' Way* in 1987: one of his Sealine

Left Chris Collman's Quay Marine power boat centre on the Hamble, known to *Howards' Way* fans as Leisurecruise. *Below left* Inside Quay Marine

Ambassadors is featured in the title credits. He also charters cruisers to the programme as camera or support vessels. Perhaps Ken could take a leaf or two out of his book; whenever Chris sells a boat to someone new to the water, the sales service includes a fortnight's course in how to drive it and how to use the navigational equipment. The courses are run by his resident skipper, Terry Jones, who keeps an eye on the new boatowner until the vessel's first service. No one's allowed simply to drive off. Recently, though, someone did; one of Chris's boats was stolen from its mooring and driven up the Hamble. It has never been seen again, despite a police helicopter search.

'The image of the motor cruiser is changing. They are faster than they used to be, and more luxurious.' This they certainly are, with cabins, bathrooms and plenty of space. Because they can now do 35–40 knots, it is possible to get to the Channel Islands in three hours from Southampton, and their owners are using them more and more for holidays – they are like marine caravans.

Chris has been involved with boats all his life, and, like Ken, has raced power boats. 'There was one time when I crashed in a race. I was thrown clear, but I literally flew out of my shoes, just like a character in a cartoon film. My feet just contracted as I braced myself for the impact.'

Howards' Way has undoubtedly stimulated interest in small boats among the public. The Elephant Yard, on the downstream side of Bursledon bridge from Quay Marine, is solid with yachts drawn up for repairs, and everywhere you look on the river there is a forest of masts. *Barracuda of Tarrant* is there too, looking rather forlorn, getting her facelift for filming. Modest though it looks, the yard provided the present firm's founder, Michael Richardson, with enough money to retire comfortably, to a yacht of his own on the Mediterranean, before *Howards' Way* came along.

Michael took over the yard in the early fifties, when he was made redundant from the aircraft industry, but the place has a much longer history than that. Astonishingly for such a small place, it was here that the frigate HMS *Elephant* was built in 1786. She became Nelson's flagship for the Battle of Copenhagen, and the yard takes its name from her. A plaque in St Leonard's Church, Bursledon, commemorates her builder, George Parsons. The yard is run now by Michael's son, Tom, who denies that their connection with *Howards' Way* has directly brought them greater prosperity. You sense his anxiety that the soberly-run and workmanlike Elephant should not be confused by serious sailing people with the more dazzling (and much more volatile) Mermaid.

To walk into the real office is to walk onto the *Howards' Way* set, except that there is no drawing-board and the only computer in sight is a modest, hardworking Amstrad. There is a clutter of papers, and photographs on the wall show some of the yard's more spectacular boats – *Green Dragon*, which was yacht of the year for two years running in the mid-seventies, and *Dragon*, which sailed in the Admiral's Cup in the early eighties. Outside, the yard is an extraordinary jumble: part wood yard, part workshop, with tall trees growing in the middle of it. Signs near the entrance warn off visitors 'except on business', and allude to guard dogs, so it's unlikely that the Richardsons are bothered by any but the most determined fans of the programme. Business is evidently thriving. There are two boats in the workshop, which has been extended to accommodate one of them, a seventy-footer whose keel was laid early in 1988, and which practically fills it. She will be all wood, and they expect to take fifteen months to complete her.

The person whose collaboration with the series has been most exciting and most enthusiastic is yacht designer Tony Castro. He has been designing yachts for more than ten years, and has run his own design company since 1982. He was born in Lisbon, and has sailed since he was a child, going to sailing school from the age of nine. Before that he preferred angling – he started when he was seven. He studied naval architecture but didn't like working on big-ship design, though he spent time in the shipyards of Sweden in their heyday; so he turned to designing yachts.

His office would appeal to Tom Howard. It is high high-tech, with ranks of computers and printers. He designed the computer graphics featured in the programme. Tony works in an inner office, which contains a large desk and a drawing-board. He has designed two boats in conjunction with *Howards' Way* and is busy designing a third. For an internationally respected designer to be so keen to work with the programme says more about its influence than words. But the collaboration has helped Tony realise a few dreams too.

He became involved through Bob Fisher, and his involvement began with Barracuda. The idea of a revolutionary new boat had occurred to Gerry at the outset of the programme, and Tony had been thinking about the same thing. A yacht with a lightweight hull, which could make the most of a smaller sail area for a forty-five footer, and would therefore be easier to handle; but which would go like the wind when you bent on more sail. A racer which could double as a comfortable cruiser. There wasn't such a boat around at the time, although now, three years later, she has started a trend.

The idea of a boat like Barracuda came to Tony during a discussion with Bob Fisher while they were taking part in the China Sea Race a couple of years ago. They were 400 miles from anywhere, somewhere between Hong Kong and Manila. 'It's a good race though not, of course, as demanding as the Round the World. But you have to look after yourself because there's no equivalent of the RNLI out there, and there's a very real danger of pirates.' Two days after we spoke, he was due to take part in this year's race, which he won for the third consecutive series.

'That day, the wind was blowing a hoolie, but our boat was only doing about nine and half knots. I just wished we were on a boat which could make more use of the wind.' A few months later, the *Howards' Way* connection provided him with precisely the opportunity he wanted to design and build the experimental boat he'd envisaged. In the normal course of events, it would have been an uphill struggle to convince any boatyard to invest the time and labour needed to realise such a project. The step was too big for the conservative British boat industry. 'It was a completely new wrapping incorporating and combining old concepts. Sailing boats have been around far too long, almost as long as man, for any really new ideas to be left. The backing of *Howards' Way* enabled us to initiate work on it. Most of the time one is interpreting other people's demands, this time our client was prepared to let us have our head.'

It took eight months from drawings to boat. Marketing it commercially was an opportunity too good to miss, quite apart from the research and development costs which needed to be defrayed. The prototype was built in wood at the Elephant Yard and then reproduced commercially by another company, Sadler's (a production-line boatmaker like Relton's). The one we see in the series is the original boat, run off-screen and on by Bob Fisher. The production model has certainly sold, but Tony thinks it should have done better. On the water, with sails, a Barracuda will set you back £150 000.

'They've sold twenty so far. If the BBC had not come along and breathed life into this project, Bob and I wouldn't have convinced anyone to do it. Even when the boat was there the reaction of the industry was surprisingly negative.' But he points out again that the marine industry is conservative. 'There are only a few innovators, and when they're successful they're "knocked". It's almost as if success were a bad word.' He didn't realise at the time what a big step Sadler's were taking in going along with him. He'd assumed that the builders would be as forward-looking as he was. It took a lot of effort to convince them to take the boat at all, 'but even when they had, they didn't appear to me to throw their full weight and enthusiasm behind it and they probably lost hundreds of thousands of pounds' worth of business. They were not ready, not positive enough. But it would have been an insurmountable job to get the Barracuda launched at all if it hadn't been for Gerry and the BBC.' They set something off which they weren't aware of, because as outsiders they could identify without prejudice neglected areas of the market, which the insiders hadn't noticed.

Spring is another new concept. She is a twenty-five footer which comes as a basic sailing boat for £12 000; but with the supplementary 'Spring packs', which comprise additional sails and an engine, she can be anything you want her to be. At eight-foot beam, she is the maximum width for towing, so she could be kept at home (thereby avoiding hefty mooring fees, which can run into thousands a year for a large boat). The

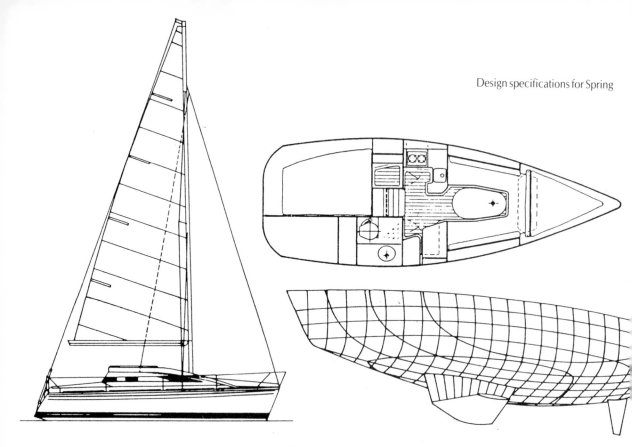

concept was Gerry Glaister's, developed through the programme as Jan's idea for a yuppie boat in series three of *Howards' Way*. Tom designs it.

'We were able to explain to the production-boat developers, MG Yachts, precisely what Spring would be and what its target market was – people who might prefer to buy a boat to a second car, but people with some money and a sense of fun. MG put up a lot of money to make it happen, and their enthusiasm has really paid off.' Personal appearances by *Howards' Way* stars at boat shows haven't done any harm either. Between September 1987 and March 1988, 150 Springs were sold. 'Alan Poole, who runs MG Yachts, was asking for a £200 deposit, but people were ringing up and buying the boat outright on their credit cards. Of course, not everybody has that kind of credit card!'

'That is an unheard of success in the British marine industry,' says Tony. 'It's the greatest success ever, and once again it has come about only because of *Howards' Way*. I don't think the boat has *sold* because of the serial, but without the back-up of the programme MG might not have put themselves behind it. MG saw that if the BBC put the boat on the screen, it might be worth their while spending some money developing it.' Of course, the BBC is not financially involved, but its weight convinced others of the viability of the design.

Spring and Barracuda share certain design features which are new, a little way out and even cheeky. But the innovations are intelligent, like the twin rudders, which mean that when the boat tilts in the water the immersed rudder digs in deeper, providing greater stability and control.

Spring represents an even bigger revolution than Barracuda because, although there are envious detractors, her success is undeniable. Even the yachting establishment are coming round to accepting her. Like Barracuda, she's a cruiser capable of racing if required but, at half the size and less than a tenth of the price, somewhat more manageable. Tony says, 'When Gerry outlined the idea to me, it was music to my ears. I began to look at how it could be developed, ways around the problems, and how it could be integrated into today's world. Given the original idea, if you get the right people working on it, there is room for many other successful projects. But if it weren't for *Howards' Way*, we wouldn't be sitting here and Spring wouldn't exist.'

Tony is now part of a syndicate designing Peter de Savary's next America's Cup boat. The America's Cup will feature fictionally in *Howards' Way* too. In the meantime, he is designing yet another boat for the series. It's a motorised fishing boat, and again it's Gerry's idea. 'It's hard to target a market for it because fishing is so much more widespread than yachting, but the potential is much bigger.'

The new boat will be called the Orcadian. It's quite small, but just big enough to have a cabin with a large double bed and a separate toilet and galley. Its cockpit is big enough to appeal to anglers, but a choice of engines will make it whatever you want: low-powered for canals, more power for rivers, and she can even be made into a speedboat. She will be robust, able to take rough treatment and stout enough for coastal sailing. 'She's being developed for us by an English company called Orkney Boats who are based at Arundel. They've only done smaller boats up to now, so this will be a big project for them.'

One boat will be built specially for the serial, in wood of course, beautifully varnished, and it will be Jack Rolfe's baby. There is a tradition for people who have bought their boats out of money made from horses to name their boat after their horse. In the serial Jack will name his boat after the filly Sir Edward gives Kate – *Spirit of Kate*. Because of his own childhood love of fishing, Tony says that he is really enjoying this project. 'It's a labour of love.' He adds, '*Howards' Way* is true to life. As far as boats are concerned, it is completely authentic. There is no doubt in my mind that the series has had a good effect on the entire British marine industry.'

There have been tangible knock-on effects in Southampton. Together with Graham Shaw of the Southampton City Directorate of Leisure, Tourism and Amenities, Gerry developed the *Howards' Way* weekends, which are held several times throughout the summer and attract hundreds of tourists to the area, not only to visit the villages where the serial is set but to see the attractions of the surrounding countryside and the New Forest. The Wolf Rock Race, which shares the same start as the Fastnet, has been revived as a result of the influence of *Howards' Way*, and the renewal of interest in Channel racers stimulated by Barracuda.

There are more overlaps between the serial and reality. Not only have the Elephant Yard offices been reproduced as sets, the bars of The Jolly Sailor have too, complete with their nautical names: the Foc's'le and the Quarter Deck (even the toilets are called Mermaids and Mariners). In the real pub, though, you can get a tremendous selection of beers served by barmaid Madge, including the wonderful Badger, which beats the cold tea served on the set. Two other pubs in the vicinity, which have not appeared on screen, are certainly worth a visit. At The Chequers in Lymington, members of the yachting fraternity gather on Sunday nights to watch *Howards' Way*, have a drink and identify their friends, who are doing the real crewing. The other place to try is The Hobbler near Brockenhurst, which one member of the *Howards' Way* team described as 'the Langan's Brasserie of the south'.

At times fiction blurs with reality. Not only has Bursledon BR station smartened itself up since the series began, it obligingly changes to Tarrant for filming. One day during a shooting session a real train drew in and two elderly ladies got out. When they saw that the station signs read Tarrant and not Bursledon, they got back in again.

Some critics have raised the objection that a man as rich as Charles Frere would not be interested in the small money to be made in the area, but in real life City man David May runs Berthon International at Lymington. He also owns Lymington Marina and Berthon Boats. The marina has moorings for several hundred boats, and fees for the average yacht are around £2000 a year. There is no reason for Charles to sneeze at that kind of investment. Frere's business park development is also based on a real development taking place in the area. Fiction and reality meet at every point.

159

What of the future of *Howards' Way*? If the saga continues, what changes will we see? One thing we can reveal is that Jan, taking her cue from fashion ski-wear, will begin to market fashion sail-wear. In real life, Henri Lloyd, the maker of perhaps the finest sail-wear in the world, is developing a line of sailing and après-sail clothes which will be designed in Italy and which will feature in *Howards' Way* as the product of Jan's fashion house. The new clothes will be worn by the Australian yachting journalist and sailor, Mike Hanley, and by Leo and Abby when they sail *Spring of Tarrant*.

But what of the others? Will Tom stay afloat financially? Will Sir Edward crush Charles? Will Polly break out at last? And will Leo lead Abby to the altar? My lips are sealed, but Gerry's head is full of ideas, enough to provide a fair wind for *Howards' Way* to sail on well into the nineties – if not into the next millennium!